Alfonso Gálvez

PRAYER

Translated from the Spanish by
Michael Adams

New Jersey
U.S.A. – 2022

CATALOGING DATA

Author: Gálvez, Alfonso, 1932–2022
Title: Prayer

First Printing   New Jersey, 1998
Second Printing   New Jersey, 2022

Library of Congress Catalog Card Number: 2020917553

ISBN: 978-1-7322886-7-6 (hardcover)
      978-1-7322886-8-3 (e-book)

**Published by
Shoreless Lake Press
P.O. Box 157
Stewartsville, New Jersey 08886**

"No longer do I call you servants… but friends…"
(Jn 15:15)

"Only one thing is necessary…"
(Lk 10:42)

INTRODUCTION

This little book is not a treatise on prayer. It has been assembled with the help of outlines or notes containing ideas which everyone is familiar with —notes which the author used for giving talks to ordinary but generous people already quite advanced in the spiritual life.

Much of what is said here can also be applied to vocal prayer, though the author is almost always referring to mental prayer; this is something one will easily notice and there is no need to repeat it.

It should be borne in mind that the true Teacher of prayer is the Holy Spirit, to whom anyone needs to have recourse if he desires to make progress in prayer. We also need to have recourse to the Blessed Virgin, an outstanding teacher of prayer, given that she was the best and most faithful hearer of the Word and, at the same time, the one whose response to it was most generous and loving —*Let it be done to me according to thy word*—; she, better than anyone, pondered on it in her heart —*Mary kept all these things in her heart*—, and she was the one who was closest to her Son and to the Spirit of her Son.

Everyone knows that prayer is a vast subject, both in importance and in range. And anything we manage to say about it will always fall too short and convey almost nothing. But let us put ourselves in God's hands, humbly and trustingly, so that He guides us along the ways that lead to that only thing necessary.

This little book is only a short vade—mecum which can be useful for reminding people of ideas they already know. To explore the subject in greater depth we have the great treatises written by the masters of the spiritual life.

THE BASES OF PRAYER

Prayer grows out of the need God has chosen to feel to speak to us —and the need we feel to speak to Him. Speaking is a form of communication, but in this context it involves a form of communication which is, above all, an outpouring of love towards the loved one. Obviously we are not saying very much when we say that prayer is a conversation between God and man. Prayer is in fact a special form of becoming aware of, and intensifying, the life of intimacy that exists between God and man. It means man becoming intimately conscious of divine–human love. Clearly, if there is no communication between lovers, no love can happen —and this also applies when the lovers are God and man.

In the Trinity, the Father *utters* to Himself what He is with just one Word, which He loves with a Love which is identical with the response He receives, that is, the Holy Spirit. Well, prayer is the prolongation *ad extra*, in man, of the dialogue that takes place in the Trinity. In prayer there is actualized, in a very special way, the fact that man has been given entry to, given a share in, the eternal and ineffable dialogue of love that takes place in the bosom of the Trinity. The mystery of prayer derives from the mystery of the goodness of God, Who chose to give man a share in His own divine life. To understand the mystery of prayer one would need to know why God chose to make man His son, friend and interlocutor by giving him His own only–begotten Son and the Spirit of His Son. The mystery of prayer is the mystery of the love God has for man.

Christian prayer is located equidistantly between two errors which seem to be opposed to one another: atheism and pantheism. Both these errors rule out the possibility of prayer because they rule out the possibility of dialogue between God and man. Atheism rules out God, in favor of man; and pantheism rules out man, in favor of God. But clearly, any type of love, even divine love, calls for there being more than one person so that there can be communication and self–giving between them. Therefore, the complete revelation of God as Perfect Love is the revelation of God as Trinity. For God is that, no more, no less: perfect Love; or, if you wish, simply Love (1 Jn 4:8).

God desires to converse with us because He loves us. Prayer is the response we give to His invitation to converse with Him; or, better to say, it is that conversation, that dialogue, actually taking place: *In many and various ways God spoke of old to our fathers by the prophets; but in these last days he has spoken to us by a Son.*[1] Because He loves us and therefore desires to communicate with us, He has spoken to us and has given us His own Word, making us His

---

[1]Heb 1: 1–2.

true interlocutors because He wants His love for us to be true. That is why He has brought us into His Son and has given us a share in His life by participation —and has also given us the Spirit to pray on our behalf, since we would not know how to go about it: *The Spirit Himself intercedes for us with sighs too deep for words.*[2]

The Son is the Father's Word, and is loved by Him in a Love which is, in turn, Love and the Son's response. That Love, which is the Spirit, is given to us so that, through Him, we might possess the Son and go in the Son to the Father, thereby sharing in the mysterious dialogue of the Trinity. The Spirit makes it possible for us to pray, which is the same as saying that He makes it possible for us to speak with God and be His friends.

This is merely a starting–off point, because prayer is much more than a dialogue between God and man. For, just as in the bosom of the Trinity the dialogue between the Father and the Son is fully achieved, perfected, and expressed in the Love that is the Spirit; just as that dialogue expresses itself in the mutual self–surrender and self–giving of the Father and the Son in the Love that is the Spirit; in the same way, and given that prayer is a calling to man to share in the Trinitarian dialogue, that divine–human dialogue is destined to reach its consummation in mutual self–giving in Love. Therefore, the Spirit in us means both the very possibility of prayer and the sign that we are already in God, in an exchange of words and mutual self–giving in love: *The Spirit himself bears witness to our spirit that we are children of God...*[3] *It will not be you who speak, but the Spirit of your Father speaking in you.*[4] Later on we shall see that the text of Romans 8:26 has to be interpreted in the

---

[2]Rom 8:26.

[3]Rom 8:16.

[4]Mt 10:20.

fullest sense: it means not only that the Spirit *intercedes for us*, which would mean *on our behalf*, but that He prays *in* us. The Spirit has been given to us so that, through Him, we can listen to and understand the Son, and, through the Spirit and in the Son, we can give a perfect response to the Father; for we have already said that the presence of the Spirit in us means that we are able to converse with God: able to hear and be heard, to understand and be understood, to love and be loved, to be gods without ceasing to be men: *I tell you the truth: it is to your advantage that I go away, for if I do not go away, the Counsellor will not come to you.*[5]

Prayer is not only dialogue, although it certainly is dialogue. Therefore, it necessarily presupposes different persons who speak and listen to one another —and who, in this case, are God and man. And for this to happen both need to have something to say —and the desire to say it. Now, as far as God is concerned, He clearly does desire to converse with man: He created him, He has made him a sharer in His own life and has in fact spoken to him and does speak to him: *In many and various ways God spoke of old to our fathers by the prophets; but in these last days he has spoken to us by a Son...*[6] *This is my beloved Son; listen to him.*[7] It is not that God now addresses men with words, but that, having sent men His own Word, in Him He has said everything and has nothing more to say, as Saint John of the Cross puts it. In the prologue to his Gospel Saint John tells us that the Word was sent to men. And our Lord Himself tells us, in the parable of the sower, about the word of God addressed to men and the different ways they receive it.

---

[5] Jn 16:7.
[6] Heb 1: 1–2.
[7] Mt 17:5.

God has spoken to us through His Son. But the Son's words, contained in Scripture and Tradition and guarded and interpreted by the Church, must then be heard by each man and given private, personal attention. Of course, we should not forget that, in order to be authentic and not lose touch with the truth, this listening and this understanding must be done in the Church and with the Church. It is here that the Spirit intervenes; were it not for His work, the so–called official revelation would never become effective in us: *The Counsellor, the Holy Spirit, whom the Father will send in my name, he will teach you all the things, and will bring to your remembrance all that I have told you.*[8] And the Spirit breathes where He wills and as He wills, without our being able to know where He comes from or where He is going to (Jn 3:8). He can reach us in very different ways and circumstances, but the normal and best way is through prayer. Prayer in this way becomes the normal mode whereby the Spirit establishes communication between God and man, by which He enables us to understand the Son's words so that through the Son we should hear the Father: *What I say I say as the Father has bidden me...*[9] *The words that I say to you I do not speak on my own authority...*[10] *He who sent me is true, and I declare to the world what I have heard from Him.*[11] And at the same time as He enables us to hear the Father, He gives us the ability to speak to Him.

It is the Spirit Who brings it about that the word of God, addressed to man, can be responded to and become intimate dialogue, which is the perfect form of communication among persons. Once again this brings us to the ineffable intimacy of the life of the Trin-

---

[8] Jn 14:26.

[9] Jn 12:50.

[10] Jn 14:10.

[11] Jn 8:26.

ity being translated into man's very life: the dialogue of man with
God is a true copy of the dialogue in the Trinity.[12] It is an intimate personal dialogue, which begins in the I and is addressed to
the Thou. Until that dialogue takes place, the Word of God will
be for men something like *the sound of many waters*.[13] Dialogue is
not something you have with a crowd; it happens intimately, in a
much closer context. Therefore, when God desired to speak to His
People, He called Moses aside to dialogue with him. The terminus
of divine speech and love is always intimacy between persons. This
is what Saint Paul was getting at when, speaking in the singular
and about Jesus Christ, he said: *He loved me and gave himself for
me*.[14] And the bride in the Song expressed the same idea when she
said: *I am my beloved's and my beloved is mine*.[15] In the end, our
Lord always says to us, as He did to the Samaritan woman: *I who
speak to you am he*;[16] or to the man born blind who asked Him who
the Son of man was: *You have seen him, and it is he who speaks
to you*.[17] Moreover, our Lord calls each of His sheep by its name
(Jn 10:3); and this calling is the ultimate, individual, intimate, and
personal expression of a consummated divine love.

---

[12]This comparison with the dialogue in the Trinity is an analogy. Bearing in
mind the differences, the dialogue and the intimacy found here are real, just as
man's participation in the divine life is real.

[13]Rev 1:15.

[14]Gal 2:20.

[15]Sg 6:3.

[16]Jn 4:26.

[17]Jn 9:37.

DIVINE–HUMAN DIALOGUE AND HUMAN COMMUNICATION

We have already referred to there being a certain analogy between divine–human dialogue —prayer— and the mysterious dialogue in the Trinity itself. But it is also true that dialogue —communication— between human being and human being is an imperfect imitation of man's dialogue with God. This means that the more intense, the better, an individual human being's dialogue with God, the better is that person able to make himself heard by others. The reason, quite often, why men fail to make themselves understood to one another may be found, among other things, in their prior and manifest inability to communicate with God. The basis of dialogue or communication between human beings is prior dialogue with God, just as the basis of love among human beings is their prior divine–human love relationship. Hence men find it impossible to make themselves understood to one another when they cease to speak to God.

Divine–human dialogue can fail on the part of the human inter-locutor, but never on the part of God. On the other hand, when it is a matter of human beings speaking to and listening to one another, dialogue can fail to result due to either of the parties involved. As far as any kind of communication among human beings is concerned, speaking in general and in a very wide sense, we can say that dia-logue can fail to result, sometimes through the fault of the listener, and at other times, perhaps more often, through the failure of the speaker. Hence our need to watch the way we set about addressing others, in order to ensure that it is not our fault that dialogue does not happen. And in order to do this, we need first to converse with God —in a dialogue which, among other things, needs to be very sincere.

This has great importance for all types of apostolate, but par-ticularly for ministerial preaching. Saint Paul used to say that he spoke to his faithful *in words taught by the Spirit*;[1] and our Lord said emphatically that He spoke to us in words He heard from the Father,[2] which seems even more logical when one remembers that, when all is said and done, He is the Word of the Father. There-fore, if one does not first listen to God and dialogue with Him, one clearly is not in a position to address men, and even less so to act as God's spokesman. The man who has learned to speak to God will be more easily listened to and understood by his fellow men: *Lucerna pedibus meis verbum tuum et lumen semitis meis*.[3] If man

---

[1] 1 Cor 2:13.
[2] Cf. Jn 14:10, etc.
[3] Ps 119:105.

does not listen to and respond to that Word, he will lose his way and cause others to go astray. That is why it was Saint Paul's desire that the Word should be given abundant hearing among the Christians at Colossae, and why he even seems to make it a prerequisite for admonishing and teaching one another: *Let the word of Christ dwell in you richly, as you teach and admonish one another in all wisdom.*[4] Saint John also seems to say that the Word must be in us if we desire to know ourselves and practice sincerity of heart: *If we say we have not sinned, we make him a liar, and his word is not in us.*[5] And he seems to lay down the same condition for young men if they are to have the virtue of fortitude and to overcome the evil one: *I write to you, young men, because you are strong and the word of God abides in you, and you have overcome the evil one.*[6] Our Lord, for His part, proclaimed as supremely blessed those who hear the word of God and keep it (Lk 11:28); adding that he who hears His word, believing in the One who sent Him, has eternal life already (Jn 5:24); indeed, He goes so far as to compare His word to a seed which, when cast on good ground, can give abundant fruit, thirty–fold, sixty–fold, or a hundred–fold (Mt 13:23).

---

[4]Col 3:16.

[5]1 Jn 1:10.

[6]1 Jn 2:14.

REJECTION OF PRAYER AND THE CRISIS OF FAITH

If there is no desire for dialogue, dialogue cannot take place; therefore, when man wants to have nothing to do with God, prayer becomes impossible and there is no room for it. In fact, this negative attitude is the only cause for the failure of prayer. At the present time we are undergoing a crisis of prayer worse probably than at any other time in History. However, the Gospel already drew attention to the attitude of demons: they rejected any type of contact or dialogue with our Lord: *What have you to do with us, O Son of God? Have you come here to torment us before the time?*[1] Indeed, it seems as if man today wants to have nothing to do with God; restless and ill at ease for various reasons, like Martha in the Gospel

---

[1]Mt 8:29.

(Lk 10:41), he seems to find himself in a situation of not being able to hear or understand God, and he even tries to justify himself by arguing that he is right. Perhaps that is why our Lord said: *Why do you not understand what I say? It is because you cannot bear to hear my word.*[2]

We are not going to examine here the arguments people use to try to justify giving up prayer, because they are well known. To counter them, all we will do is recall the fact that prayer is necessary. In the book of the Acts of the Apostles we are told that the Apostles —who had shared the Master's life and had received the Spirit in abundance— came to see that it did not make sense for them to devote themselves exclusively to waiting at tables, *for we should devote ourselves to prayer and to the ministry of the word.*[3] Two points might be made in this connection. The first refers to the fact that prayer is mentioned in the first place, even before the ministry of the word. The second is that the activity referred to in the text, when it talks about serving at tables, is clearly an exercise of charity, yet it says that is not reason enough.

The contemporary crisis of prayer is an aspect of the contemporary crisis of faith. Perhaps each of these crises conditions the other. Very often preaching is devoid of supernatural content and no longer seems to echo a word spoken by God which was hearkened to before being passed on. Saint Paul, as he himself said, taught with words *taught him by the Spirit.* But many preachers today prefer rather to learn from the world, scrutinizing certain *signs of the times* which, according to them, give a better insight into the authentic content of Revelation. And so they adopt the attitude of judging and of explaining the world by means of the world itself, which is why their

---

[2] Jn 8:43.

[3] Acts 6: 2–4.

word, instead of being the word of God, is a purely human word. This sort of preaching ends up being worldly, in the sense that it is always talking about the things of the world and, moreover, doing so from a purely worldly perspective: *They are of the world; therefore what they say is of the world, and the world listens to them.*[4] In one of the earliest texts of Christian literature we read the following: *"They," said he, "are faithful, and he who is sitting on the chair is a false prophet, who is corrupting the understanding of the servants of God. He corrupts the understanding of the double-minded, not of the faithful. These double-minded men come to him as to a wizard, and ask him concerning their future; and the false prophet, having no power of the Divine Spirit in himself, speaks with them according to their requests, and according to the desires of their wickedness, and fills their souls as they themselves wish. He is empty and makes empty answers to empty men; for whatever question is put he answers according to the emptiness of the man who puts it. But he also speaks some true words, for the devil fills him with his spirit, to see if he can break any of the righteous."*[5]

The false prophet, then, puts on doctrinal airs and projects an image of confidence, using his own doctrine, which is independent and quite different from that of the Magisterium of the Church —he is seated in the master's chair—, and the destruction he wreaks on the servants of God begins at the doctrinal level. However, the faithful he destroys are not true believers, but waverers; or those who, in their heart of hearts, have already opted to be against God. These waverers, although they have already opted for selfishness, are nevertheless still looking for some sort of security: that is why they put questions to the false prophet as if he were some sort of

---

[4] 1 Jn 4:5.

[5] *Shepherd of Hermas. Eleventh Commandment.*

oracle. The replies he gives are false, in line with their own malice and what they want to hear. He does not tell them the truth. Yet he still mouths truths also, but in a mysterious mingling of half–truths and falsehoods, which gives a semblance of truth to his luring words, the better to deceive his hearers, whoever they may be. In the face of that sort of behaviour, the true believer has only one recourse, that of humble obedience to the true Church and the practice of prayer.

Rejection of prayer is in line with opting for a kind of *philosophy of praxis* at the base of which lies Marxist ideology. As we know, Marxism regards philosophy as having served no purpose hitherto, because it has not changed man. Work is the only thing that makes man truly human —not speculation or contemplation. Instead of contemplating the world, what one must do is become active, to change it. In Catholic theology there was never any contradiction between action and contemplation, despite some less than happy exegesis of Luke 10: 41–42 which sought to exalt the value of prayer to the detriment of action. In the saints one always found a well–rounded, perfect synthesis of action and contemplation, elements which are not only not opposed to one another but never can be. Nowadays this matter is no longer at issue on the speculative level, but it is in practice because many people have opted for action and given up contemplation. This has led, within Catholicism, to the development of pastoral action of a purely human kind —which only proves that the salt of the Gospel has become insipid and the cross has been drained of its strength. This was the only logical outcome of a certain psychological inferiority complex, and of what is called *disincarnation* vis–à–vis the world, that the Church is suffering from today.

THE PRACTICE OF PRAYER

Prayer is at one and the same time easy and difficult. It is easy, because prayer is simply a dialogue and an outpouring of love between God and man. But, because man is wounded by sin, certain things have become difficult for him which should always have been easy. The practice of prayer is one such thing.

Apprenticeship to prayer lasts one's whole life, so no one is ever in a position to say that he knows prayer inside out. True prayer is always a mystery for one who practices it. There is nothing surprising about this if one remembers that the intimacy of divine–human dialogue is quite ineffable: only God knows the depths of the Spirit, and those of the human heart (Rom 8:27; 1 Cor 2:10; Ps 7:10; Jer 17:10; Rev 2:23). Therefore, one would be quite wrong to think that all one had to know were the rules given by the mystics, often very detailed rules, in order to work out where exactly one was on the road of prayer.[1]

The problem of the difficulty of prayer is part of the problem of the difficulties involved in living the faith seriously. Besides, there is a mutual relationship between prayer and genuine Christian living, so much so that each impacts the other. This is true of the sort of prayer we might call "prayer of beginners," which should be the normal thing for every Christian. For, if we are dealing with the more advanced practice of prayer, we find even greater difficulties, even very serious ones, which can call for heroism if one is to overcome them and which the common run of Christians are completely unaware of.

Clearly there is as little justification for discouragement in the face of these difficulties as there is for discouragement in the face of the difficulties one must overcome to live a serious Christian life. And since prayer is necessary if one genuinely wants to live according to the teachings of Jesus Christ, one needs to be ready to practice it and to strive to get others to do the same. One needs to do this to the extent that one wants Christian life to become a reality. If an apostle does not make teaching the life of prayer one of the goals of his activity, then perhaps the reason is that his own prayer–life is a failure —and that must mean that his Christian life over all is a failure. A priest, for example, one of whose missions is that of teaching his flock how to pray, shows himself to be lukewarm, lacking in faith, or a coward in the face of the cross if he does not perform that teaching role. It would be a very grave matter if that

---

[1]We are not denying the usefulness of the mystics' teachings on prayer. What we are saying is that a purely theoretical knowledge of prayer seems impossible. And that these rules, on their own, are not very helpful for working out where exactly a person is on the road of prayer. Here, as in so many other places, only God can produce exact measurements.

happened, because our world is more than ever in need of people who pray.

SILENCE

Prayer needs silence, both exterior and interior. Prior to sin, man conversed with God as a matter of course; but, after the Fall, it became more difficult for him to hear the voice of God. Things became more real for man than the presence of God, and the noise of things began to be heard with more force than the voice of the Creator.

Our Lord sought silence when He wanted to pray. That was why He went off into the hills (Lk 6:12; 22:39), or the desert (Mt 4; Mk 1; Lk 4); He took Himself off in the early morning (Mk 1:35), or else at night (Mt 14:23), combining the solitude of the place with the proper hour, as these texts show.

Because things are good in themselves, there is no reason why they should separate us from God. But since man is a disturbed being, he runs the risk of immersing himself in things in a disordered way, never getting beyond them, never reaching God. Besides, even if there were no disorder of any kind in us, as was the case of our Lord, we would still be in need of solitude and silence in order to converse with God, at least at some points in the day. This is so because He wants us to recognize Him as the Lord of things and as Someone totally distinct from things. And it would be very difficult for us to do that if we did not, for some moments in the day, sacrifice things, distancing them from our cares and worries in order to turn ourselves towards God and listen quietly to His voice. Leaving things to one side and immersing them in silence, even if only for a few moments, acts as a kind of sacrifice which prepares us to listen to the voice of God. This is the point at which He speaks to us in silence: *And he said: "Go forth, and stand upon the mount before the Lord." And behold, the Lord passed by, and a great and strong wind rent the mountains, and broke in pieces the rocks before the Lord, but the Lord was not in the wind; and after the wind an earthquake, but the Lord was not in the earthquake; and after the earthquake a fire, but the Lord was not in the fire; and after the fire a still small voice. And when Elijah heard it, he wrapped his face in his mantle and went out and stood at the entrance of the cave. And behold, there came a voice to him.*[1] The noise raised by the things of the world, which can undoubtedly stun us, is dispelled by the voice of God, which is what causes us to understand all things (Jn 14:26; 16:13). The power of that voice silences other noises and gives them their true meaning. The Gospel tells us that the clamour which announced the approaching of the Bridegroom was heard at midnight: *At midnight there was a cry, "Behold, the bridegroom!*

---

[1] 1 Kings 19: 11–13.

Come out to meet him." [2] But midnight is the quietest time of all; the point furthest away both from the end of the day and from its beginning, the dawn, as Saint John of the Cross pointed out; and it is at that very hour that the Bridegroom arrives. The Psalmist, too, chooses the quiet hours to speak to God: *Et meditatus sum nocte cum corde meo.* [3] For the voice of God, heard in the silence of prayer, is what makes everything plain and gives everything its true meaning, its proper place. It is the voice of Wisdom, or Wisdom itself, reaching us in this silence: *While gentle silence enveloped all things, and night in its swift course was now half gone, the all–powerful word leaped from heaven, from the royal throne, into the midst of the land that was doomed, a stern warrior.* [4] That is how Wisdom comes to abide with us and in us, causing us to understand and discern all things (1 Cor 2:15), which has nothing to do with the possession of human knowledge, which, on its own, is quite useless (1 Cor 8:1; 13:8). [5]

Hence our need to seek out silence, especially at certain points in the day, to be able to hear the voice of the Lord. It is said that Petrarch went up a mountain alone and there, contemplating the landscape, he realized that man is the centre of all things. We, too, when we reflect in silence, tend to see ourselves as the centre of the universe. However, with the help of the light of prayer, we do not stop there, we see that God is the center of that center: abiding closer to me than I am myself, as Saint Augustine put it. For the light of prayer adds authentic wisdom to the insights that mere

---

[2] Mt 25:6.

[3] Ps 77:6.

[4] Wis 18: 14–15.

[5] Gilson said that these our times are times with plenty of knowledge but very little wisdom. *Linguístique et Philosophie. Essai sur les constantes philosophiques du Language*, Paris, 1969.

humanism provides. If he does not have this light, man runs the risk of being de–centered, of thinking that he is the only center of the world and never managing to get to know himself. For, although in prayer God speaks to us mainly about Himself, He also speaks to us about ourselves, who, in the last analysis, are made in His image and likeness. In the quietness and in the silence of prayer the Spirit speaks to us of Jesus, Whose knowledge man must first acquire if he ever wants to know himself.

But man today hardly knows what silence is. And, what is worse, he flees from it, because he cannot abide being alone with himself. Like Adam, he is afraid to hear in the silence of the evening the voice of God calling to him (Gen 3:8), and therefore he also hides away. Modern man's fear of silence is a fear of being face to face with himself and, in the last analysis, a fear of hearing the voice of God.

There is a time to be silent and a time to speak, Ecclesiastes tells us. This time for silence is certainly a time for men to quieten all dealings among themselves, for it is a time to speak to God. There is a time for speaking to our fellow men, and there is also a time for immersing ourselves in silence in order there to hear the voice of God. The Song of Songs speaks to us about the coming of the Bridegroom in the peace of nocturnal rest:

> *Open to me, my sister, my love,*
> *my dove, my perfect one;*
> *for my head is wet with dew,*
> *my locks with the dew of the night.*[6]

Every day we need to distance ourselves from our everyday tasks, at least for a while, in order to concentrate on listening to the voice

---

[6]Sg 5:2.

of God in silence: *And he said to them: "Come away by yourselves to a lonely place, and rest awhile." For many were coming and going, and they had no leisure even to eat.*[7]

Modern man always finds reasons to object to all this. There's no time. Besides, one can turn his life into prayer. But it always boils down to the same thing: things are what matter; there is no point in allocating time exclusively for speaking to God. Anyway, finding time to devote exclusively to prayer is not a matter of having time to spare (an intelligent person never has time on his hands, given that boredom is a privilege of fools); it is a matter of being convinced that one must seek out that time. And a person will always find it if he is convinced there is a real need to. Ecclesiastes already told us so long ago: *For everything there is a season, and time for every matter under heaven.*[8]

---

[7]Mk 6:31.
[8]Eccles 3:1.

ENEMIES OF SILENCE: DISTRACTIONS

It is much easier to achieve exterior silence than interior silence. We are all well aware that worries, memories, and imagination can be a considerable distraction. Saint Teresa described imagination as the mad woman of the house; sometimes it is better just to let her be and pay her no attention. And there is no doubt but that the various concerns caused by our daily activities can become a serious obstacle to prayer:

> *Catch us the foxes,*
> *the little foxes,*
> *that spoil the vineyards,*
> *for our vineyards are in blossom.*[1]

---

[1] Sg 2:15.

The struggle against distractions in prayer affects our whole day, and not just the time allotted for prayer. One needs to make a genuine effort to practice the presence of God right through the day, and to ask humbly for interior peace, which is a fruit of the Holy Spirit (Gal 5:22). If we make this effort, the transition from daily activity to prayer will go fairly smoothly; otherwise it would be impossible. Therefore it is absolutely necessary to keep our imagination and senses under control throughout the whole day; for reasons we know well, these factors make the life of prayer especially difficult for people today.

THE SEARCH FOR SILENCE: STRUGGLING
AGAINST DISTRACTIONS

At least during the early stages of the life of prayer, it is very helpful to use a book when praying. This book should preferably be the Bible, especially the New Testament. For, since prayer is conversation with God, it makes sense that His voice should reach us through the book whose author is the Holy Spirit, that is, the One who will enable us to have a deep understanding of it in our personal prayer. Of course, we should never forget that the Church alone has the role of authenticating the Spirit, and there can be no private teaching that contradicts the public teaching backed by the Magisterium's guarantee.

The help of a book will be needed for quite a while, perhaps for years; and it could well be that it can never be dispensed with

entirely. At least that is the normal thing, apart from when God
chooses to lead people along exceptional ways. If one gives up using a book too early on, the result can be barren prayer. However,
that does not mean one should keep on using a book when it is no
longer necessary; for, when all is said and done, reading is merely
a help to prayer, and God stands in no need of anything to communicate with those He loves. Besides, we know well that love, as
it acquires perfection, ceases to rely on intermediaries; it does not
even need words. There are two dangerous extremes to be avoided
here. Firstly, one should never hasten to give up using a book in the
mistaken belief that one has reached a level which one has in fact
not attained. As against that, one should not be afraid to give up
utilizing books when the right time comes. Naturally it is always a
good idea to seek the guidance of a good spiritual director, because
this matter involves the classical problem of the difference between
meditation and contemplation, a matter we shall examine in due
course.

One needs to be careful not to turn prayer into a reading session.
Since prayer is a loving conversation between God and man, it necessarily means that both parties must speak and listen. A person
who goes no further than reading does listen, but he does not reply;
at best he reflects or dialogues with himself. And although what is
contained in the Bible is certainly the word of God, there is need,
additionally, for the Spirit to cause the word to penetrate our heart,
transcending the letter of the text (2 Cor 3:6). It is not enough to
have encountered the voice of the Spirit, no matter how authentic
that voice be; we could still be ignorant as to where He came from or
where He was going to (Jn 3:8) or what He wanted us to do. True,
the Spirit can work directly on the soul, with or without the aid of
reading matter, and in fact He does so frequently. But in prayer it

is better to open the heart and listen, in the tranquillity of silence, to what the Spirit wants to tell us, reaching way beyond the letter, beyond human language, and even beyond our mental images and concepts. Otherwise, what our Lord warned us about could happen: that we read the word but fail to understand it, and then the devil is quick to snatch it from our heart (Mt 13:19). According to our Lord, His word bears fruit in us when, in addition to hearing it, we understand it (Mt 13:23) or receive it, as he also says in another place (Mk 4:20). Moreover, if God addresses man, He does so because He expects a reply; for if He speaks to us He does so out of love, and love always expects a response from the loved one. That is why He complains if that response is not forthcoming: *Why, when I came, was there no man? When I called, was there no one to answer?*[1] And the Bridegroom addresses the bride in the Song, demanding a loving response:

> *O you who dwell in the gardens,*
> *let me hear your voice!*[2]

Let me hear your voice! If God goes so far as to solicit love from man, it means that all human smallness is wiped away forever. If God desires to hear our voice, to hear us describe our deepest feelings, to make our problems His, to turn our life into His and His into ours (Gal 2:20), we are in the presence of Joy and nothing matters anymore, not even our wretchedness. For God has taken His place alongside us, to become intimate with us: *The Teacher is here and is calling for you.*[3] This way we come to see, to our enormous

---

[1] Is 50:2.

[2] Sg 8:13.

[3] Jn 11:28.

surprise, that there exists One for Whom we are important, One who can fill our heart —which is always so hungry for tenderness, and can never get its fill—: and for Whom the mediocrity and unimportance that the world sees in us do not apply, because He ransomed us with His life. So, from the moment when God considered man fit to be His friend and intimate, no one on this earth can ever regard himself as small or mediocre or boring.

However, with a book or without it, it will sometimes be impossible to avoid distractions. Saint Teresa was of the view that sometimes it is even an advantage to let that madwoman of the house, the imagination, rove wherever it wants. For the path of prayer does take one through some very difficult terrain. But we shall discuss this later.

THE IMITATION OF CHRIST

Prayer becomes very difficult, if not impossible, when it is not accompanied by a genuine desire to imitate Christ. And, in turn, the imitation of Christ is impossible without prayer. Each is dependent on the other. So we shall now speak about the imitation of our Lord as something which is always linked to the normal development of a life of prayer.

This does not mean that a Christian must already be a good imitator of Jesus Christ if he is to advance in prayer, much less when he is just beginning to practice prayer. The imitation of Christ is a goal more to be aimed at than one already attained; in fact, no one can ever say that he has already reached that goal: *I do not*

run aimlessly...[1] *So run that you may obtain it...*[2] *Not that I have
already obtained this or am already perfect; but I press on to make
it my own, because Christ Jesus has made me his own. Brethren,
I do not consider that I have made it my own; but one thing I
do, forgetting what lies behind and straining forward to what lies
ahead, I press on toward the goal for the prize of the upward call
of God in Christ Jesus.*[3] Our Lord is always, therefore, a goal to
be attained. Moreover, even if we had already reached that goal,
we would still be on the way, because that is how He described
Himself —*I am the Way*[4]—, adding that the only ultimate goal is
the Father (Mt 5:48; Jn 14:2ff). One does not need to be perfect to
do true prayer. On the other hand, if one desires to make progress
in prayer, one absolutely needs to have a genuine desire to imitate
Jesus. For, a close relationship with God is unthinkable unless one
possesses the Spirit, as we have already seen. But the Spirit is the
Spirit of the Son as well as the Spirit of the Father, and therefore
He is possessed only by someone whose life produces the fruits of
Christian living (Gal 5:22). The theology of the gifts also tells us
that the life of prayer does not attain perfection without the aid
of those subtle, delicate gifts which equip man to do supernatural
things in a superhuman way; and those gifts, in turn, come from
Him Who is Himself a Gift, the Gift par excellence, the Holy Spirit
(Jn 4:10; 7:39).

If Christian life is absent, the Spirit of Christ is not in us, and
without the Spirit of Christ prayer is not possible. Saint John con-
veys this beautifully in a passage of his Gospel: *He who has the*

---

[1] 1 Cor 9:26.

[2] 1 Cor 9:24.

[3] Phil 3: 12–14.

[4] Jn 14:6.

bride is the bridegroom; the friend of the bridegroom, who stands and hears him, rejoices greatly at the bridegroom's voice; therefore this joy of mine is now full.[5] So, the friend of the bridegroom hears the bridegroom's voice; and he hears it because he is with the bridegroom, he is at his side, for otherwise how could he hear it? Our Lord makes it very clear: to hear His voice one needs to be of the truth (Jn 18:37); only he who belongs to God hears the words of God (Jn 8:47). Saint Paul, too, considers that the life of prayer is impossible without the Spirit: *The Spirit helps us in our weakness; for we do not know how to pray as we ought, but the Spirit himself intercedes for us with sighs too deep for words.*[6] So, Saint Paul recognizes that we do not know how to pray, and we should surely take this statement in its strictest sense: left to ourselves, we cannot pray. This echoes what our Lord said: *Apart from me you can do nothing,*[7] or, if you wish, it repeats what the Apostle said in another place: *I want you to understand that no one can say "Jesus is Lord" except in the Holy Spirit.*[8] This impossibility of prayer does not refer to some particular level of prayer, as if to say that we cannot attain a high level of prayer through our own efforts alone. It goes much further than that and touches on something fundamental, because we do not even know what is good for us, much less how to go about asking for it. Saint Paul blames our weakness for this —he must mean, of course, our moral weakness, but also our absolute incapacity to gain access to the supernatural sphere without the help of God.

---

[5] Jn 3:29.
[6] Rom 8:26.
[7] Jn 15:5.
[8] 1 Cor 12:3.

However, by a happy paradox this obstacle actually becomes something for us to glory in. Because then the Spirit Himself comes to our aid and acts as our advocate. And since that Spirit is the Spirit of Christ, we can once again conclude that we cannot pray unless we live the life of Christ. He prays for us if He is in us: in its fullest sense this means that He really lends us His power and His voice to enable us to address the Father: in the Son, through the Holy Spirit, we address the Father. That is how we come to participate in the dialogue of the Trinity. The Spirit inserts us in the Son and makes us true sons (1 Jn 3:1). That is why the Apostle said: *For you did not receive the spirit of slavery to fall back into fear, but you have received the spirit of sonship enabling us to cry out 'Abba, Father!' The Spirit himself joins with our spirit to bear witness that we are the children of God.*[9] So the Spirit prays in us, with us, and for us, which does not mean that we have attained perfection, for it is our very weakness that the Spirit is coming to support. Our Lord referred to this in His conversation with the Samaritan woman: true worshippers, such as the Father seeks, will worship *in Spirit and truth;*[10] this is a text in which our Lord is probably referring not so much to spiritual worship (obviously all worship is spiritual) as to a worship of the Father which takes place precisely in the bosom of the Spirit, in Whom the praying person lives. Saint Jude seems to imply the same thing: *But you, beloved, build yourselves up on your most holy faith; pray in the Holy Spirit; keep yourselves in the love of God.*[11] And our Lord clearly teaches

---

[9] Rom 8: 15–16.

[10] Jn 4: 23–24.

[11] Jude 20–21.

this in another passage from Saint Matthew: *It is not you who speaks, but the Spirit of your Father speaking through you.*[12]

The life of prayer calls for a genuine desire to live according to the Spirit of Jesus, and any technique, no matter what it is, will prove quite useless if it does not have this as its foundation. This means that any failure in the life of prayer usually implies that there has been a prior failure in the person's Christian life. For there is no way we can try to attain a communion of love with the Father, through the Spirit, if we do not have a communion of life with the Son made man. Prayer is communication, communion, a mutual outpouring of love, a loving dialogue, mutual self–surrender and self–giving, and a total interchange of lives; all of which is impossible if the lives of the persons concerned are at odds with or strangers to one another. The life of a person who prays is a reflection of his prayer, and his prayer is a reflection of the life he leads; it follows that a life of prayer is inconceivable without a genuine effort to live as a Christian. Firstly, because a genuine life of prayer always results in a Christian life; but also because unless a person is striving to live to be a Christian he cannot even give a thought to the idea of prayer: *The unspiritual man does not receive the gifts of the Spirit of God, for they are folly to him, and he is not able to understand them because they need to be spiritually discerned.*[13] Here the Apostle is saying two things important to our theme. Firstly, he says that the unspiritual man cannot perceive the things that come from the Spirit of God (in the preceding verse he was talking about the Spirit's teachings); and, secondly, he goes further and adds that, even when he does perceive them, they seem to be crazy —they seem inappropriate, unreasonable, and out of place; literally, the stuff of madmen.

---

[12]Mt 10:20.

[13]1 Cor 2:14.

We should stress that by this we do not mean that prayer is something exclusive to true Christians. If that were the case, we would immediately come up against the difficulty of identifying who true Christians are; and there is no one who would dare to claim to be a true disciple of our Lord, because the best disciple is in fact the one who least makes such claims. Therefore, waiting until one is perfect before one begins a life of prayer would be the same as condemning oneself never to begin. All that is needed is good will and a genuine desire to imitate our Lord. The tendency to think that prayer is something for the privileged few has done a lot of damage down the centuries in the history of the Church. The same has happened as regards certain virtues (such as poverty, for example) upon which people have not always worked out a genuine spirituality which manages to make them fit all the circumstances and conditions of the life of Christians in the Church. The fact is that prayer is for everyone —and we are, of course, referring to mental prayer—, just as poverty and chastity are for everyone; although then each individual will practice these things in the style and manner proper to his state in life. Prayer is not something which the perfect do; it is something a person does in order to become perfect. Or, at any rate, to become better. For, one of the effects prayer has on man is that it causes him to see how far away he is from perfection: exactly the same distance as he is away from Jesus Christ. The purpose of prayer is, in fact, to try to imitate Jesus Christ, and trying to imitate Him is the way one learns to pray. Two lovers come to understand each other in a communion of words and loves when their lives, their behavior, and activities converge to form a communion.

MORTIFICATION AND PRAYER

What we are going to say now follows from what we said previously, once it is clear that the imitation of Christ is a requirement for a life of prayer. The path a disciple of our Lord takes is the way of the cross.

Here, also, it is true that the development of the life of prayer is directly related to the extent of personal self–denial; prayer and mortification, in fact, condition one another. Without mortification there is no progress in prayer, and the Christian who does not pray will never decide to mortify himself. Mortification is one of the obstacles that often gets in the way of a life of prayer, and it also is, again, a proof that the Christian life is one single whole composed of parts which cannot be separated from one another. On the other hand, the life of prayer, at least at some stages in its development, necessarily involves a special participation in our Lord's cross which can be quite marked at the higher levels of prayer, as we shall see later. We are not going to discuss here the performance of personal duties, though this could be regarded as the primary, most basic kind of mortification; there can be no genuine prayer if one neglects those responsibilities. One assumes that a person who has truly made up his mind to practice prayer has that side of things under control.

As regards the right posture to adopt for prayer, it must be said that, in principle, any respectful posture is acceptable. Everyone is familiar with Saint Ignatius of Loyola's remark about it being quite possible to pray *lying down.* Certainly, it would be too venturesome to establish any fixed rule in favour of any one particular prayer posture. This is a matter which circumstances will decide, and therefore we shall simply make a few tentative points.

We should not forget that posture is an aid to prayer, and that prayer itself is a means of achieving union with God. But mere means should be kept in their place —and they are not if one forgets that they are subordinate to their end, and that the better they are, the better they help towards that end. That is why we say that any respectful posture can be good for prayer. Granted this, it is also true that certain kinds of posture can make for greater progress in prayer, and, depending on circumstances, some can be better than others. For example, kneeling would appear to be the best posture for prayer because we have already said that prayer is a particular way of sharing in our Lord's cross and is therefore very closely linked to mortification. Moreover, supplication is a basic element in Christian prayer, an element which is particularly important for those whose ministry is apostolate; and it should not be forgotten that supplication which is accompanied by a greater sharing in Jesus Christ's cross has more influence on God. This is a point disputed by those who confuse fruitful prayer with fervent prayer, forgetting that the two do not always go hand in hand and that it is impossible for us to know what fruit we gain from prayer. It can happen that difficult prayer is more beneficial for the person praying, or for others. In fact, personal prayer —sometimes, rather unhappily, called *private* prayer— always has some impact on the other members of the Mystical Body. Prayer always has an impetrating value which affects others and which is essential to it. If one were to forget this, one's prayer would degenerate into a *pious* practice that is a mere caricature of true prayer. The priest, who is specially consecrated to intercede on behalf of the people, should give special attention to the way he prays and to how he integrates into his prayer his participation in our Lord's cross; his prayer always refers to others, in one way or another. When Moses prayed to God during the Israelites' battle with Amalek, his men prevailed in the battle as long as he kept his hands raised; but when tiredness forced him to lower them, the tide turned in the Amalekites' favour.[1]

Sometimes it is not possible to do prayer kneeling down. Leaving aside the case of illness, kneeling is not a good idea when tension or fatigue make prayer more difficult. Be that as it may, a person who does prayer should remember, depending on circumstances and his own generosity and love, that prayer is always better the more mortified he is. Of course, he should never forget that mortification adds value to prayer only to the extent that mortification is the expression of greater love, because love is the key to all Christian life.

---

[1] Cf. Ex 17.

We should say the same about the most suitable time for prayer. In principle, any time of the day is good, although there is no doubt that the first hours of the day or the evening hours are most appropriate. tThe Gospel tells us that our Lord used to pray very early in the morning and sometimes during the night. Clearly our Lord was trying to get as much solitude and silence as possible, but undoubtedly this also points to an attitude of greater sacrifice and greater love: in addition to the merit derived from mortifying one's sleep, we see a desire to seek out times which do not take from one's ordinary work and, therefore, do not lessen one's self–surrender to others.

Constant mortification of the imagination and the sight and vigilance about one's reading material are necessary for the life of prayer, which can develop only in a setting of peace of heart and interior serenity.

What one reads raises important questions. Due to the abundance of publications, one generally needs to be very selective and, given that there is no time even to read good things, it would be a serious matter if we were to read bad things —and in addition it would spell the ruin of one's life of prayer. Special care needs to be taken with books which contain teaching against the faith or which are a danger to chastity; there is so much of this sort of material and it is not always easy for an untrained person to distinguish good from bad doctrine. As far as reading newspapers is concerned, all that need be said is that, even though a Christian ought to be a man of his time, he should not read without discernment any kind of press, for obvious reasons; besides, he also needs here to practice a veritable ascesis if he wants to make progress in the life of prayer. The same applies to public entertainment in general (so abundant and available to people nowadays) and to television.

Mortification at meals is particularly important as far as the life of prayer is concerned. It is interesting to read Saint Augustine's rather nice thoughts on this subject.[2] Spiritual writers generally agree that mortification in eating and drinking in addition to its ascetical and supplicatory value helps a person to keep a rein on his sensuality and gives his spirit more agility —which helps to make prayer easier. Certainly, if a Christian wants to make a real commitment to a life of prayer, he must not shirk the question of mortification in food and drink. The fast and abstinence of times gone by is almost just a memory, and for many Christians it is a closed book. On the matter of food, the modern world is one of contrasts: those who eat little, not by choice but because they have nothing else to eat; and those who eat too much and don't want to hear anything about moderation in eating except in connection with keeping their good looks. Moreover, in rich countries children are brought up in total ignorance of any kind of asceticism in eating —yet that is a necessary part of their good human education, apart altogether from supernatural considerations.

Mortification of sleep is also necessary in the life of prayer. It is not a matter of sleeping very little and then finding, during the day, that one cannot do one's duties properly. Basically, one should get all the sleep one needs, and no more. In fact, if one indulges oneself as regards sleep, one tends to be sleepy and not think clearly during the rest of the day. Besides, a person who sleeps too much will only with difficulty find time for the practice of prayer, unless he eats into the time which should be allocated to the performance of his duties. As regards supernatural motivations, which are always the most important, all we need do is refer to the absolute need to share in our Lord's cross if we genuinely want to advance in the life of prayer.

---

[2] Cf. *Confessions*, X, 31.

Mortification in one's dealings with others is also necessary. We are not referring here to charity —considered in its positive aspect and taking into account its wide range of influence as a capital virtue of Christian life—, or to the need for that virtue in order to pray. Charity's role in the Christian life is self–evident. What we are referring to here is the normal, everyday practice of daily life, especially as regards our own self–sacrificing in our dealings with others. The reasons are obvious. No one can aspire to friendship and intimacy with God unless he also practices them with those around him, because we cannot love God, Whom we cannot see, unless we also love our neighbour, whom we do see and who is by our side (1 Jn 4:20). Saint Peter exhorted husbands to love and honor their wives —and he gave them a reason: that your prayers may not be hindered (1 Pet 3:7). Besides, charity and prayer always go hand in hand, in such a way that progress in either inevitably means progress in the other. We already said something about this when dealing with the parallelism between progress in prayer and progress in the Christian life. In the last analysis charity is the soul of the Christian life and can be a good indicator of the quality of our prayer.

In addition to all this, the man of prayer needs to practice many other mortifications, internal as well as external, for, as we have said, prayer is impossible without mortification of mind and body. Without mortification, one's spirit will not be agile enough to raise itself up to pray, nor will one's body cooperate in that practice. That will happen even if one has good will —if you can say someone has good will who does not use the resources available to him and who forgets that the Spirit is ready, yes, but the flesh is still weak: Matthew 26:41. Given that man is a substantial unity of body and soul, when he prays he prays with everything he has, with his soul and with his body; and therefore the difficulties and glories of the former always echo the difficulties and the glories of the latter.

MEDITATION AND CONTEMPLATION
DISTINGUISHED

In almost everything said so far, we have been referring mainly to mental prayer or what some people call "meditation." As regards vocal prayer, if we want to distinguish it from mental prayer, it suffices here to say that vocal prayer focuses on fixed forms of words whereas mental prayer gives one's spontaneity free rein.

But mental prayer in turn divides into two types of prayer, which writers usually describe as meditation and contemplation. There are other classifications and terminologies (which can be looked up in any treatise) but here we shall confine ourselves to saying something about the connection between these two kinds of prayer.

There would appear to be essential differences, not just differences of degree, between meditation and contemplation. According to some, a person's role in meditation is rather an active one,

whereas in contemplation it is mainly passive or receptive. Others
say that in meditation it is the mind that does the work (drawing
water from the well, as Saint Teresa put it); whereas in contemplation one is taught directly by the Spirit (the rain water that
falls and makes it unnecessary to go and draw water from the well
—Saint Teresa again). All these criteria of distinction, and many
others that could be offered, are perfectly valid —but not in an absolute sense, and therefore they should not be taken too literally.
The whole matter is really much more complicated —as one might
expect, given that prayer is such a complex thing and very dependent on the supernatural. We might mention that Saint John of
the Cross provides us with an excellent doctrine on this subject; he
offers criteria for distinguishing meditation from contemplation and
identifying the point when one moves over from one to the other.[1]

It is not right to say —baldly— that a person's attitude in meditation is rather active. Clearly the Spirit has an active role to play in
meditation, not to mention the absolute need of grace everyone has
(we are referring here to prayer that has supernatural value; later
we shall say something about the prayer of the unrighteous man).
And if one says that it is a question of degree, in the sense that in
meditation man has the active role in the main, the difficulties do
not go away. In the world of things supernatural, which is where
we are at this point, it does not make sense ever to say that the
initiative lies with man. The truth is that God has His own ways
of working, and sometimes He acts on man in a very human sort of
way —which is in fact what happens here.

As regards the assertion that man's role in contemplation is
somewhat passive, that does not seem to be very felicitous. For,
since prayer is dialogue, loving communication, and mutual self-

---

[1] Cf. especially Book II of the *Ascent of Mount Carmel*, Chap. 13.

giving, it is not easy to see how all this can go on if either one of the parties is passive.

We probably have to look elsewhere for the solution to this question. In meditation man dialogues with God; he does so in a human way but grace raises him to a supernatural level. God influences man by acting on his normal human psychological make–up. In contemplation, on the other hand, the Spirit intervenes in a much more direct manner with His gifts, which exert an influence on man and cause him to act in a way which is not only supernatural but also superhuman. In contemplation the infused virtues are raised to a high degree of perfection, and at the same time man senses that he has been inserted into the world of the supernatural and has been raised far beyond where he could reach on his own, further, even, than he could have ever imagined.

The initiative never lies with man, not even in the very simplest form of prayer. Even a person who is not devout needs at least actual grace to be able to address God. But his prayer, born of the dual action of actual grace and human co–operation, will undoubtedly be listened to.

This also brings up the question of "collision." Due to the fact that each affects the other, meditation or contemplation is seldom found in a pure state, and it can be very difficult to know which is which. Purely meditative prayer, which bears no trace of contemplation, is quite rare. The same holds for contemplation: at least at the early stage it often changes into simple meditation. The path leading from meditation to contemplation is a discontinuous line; there can be points when the process stops or even goes into reverse.

Besides, there is nothing to prevent a life of prayer beginning with some kind of contemplation; in fact that seems to be fairly normal in the spiritual itinerary. True, we are referring to a very rudimentary type of contemplation which will need to be purified, but that does not mean it cannot reach a certain degree of intensity.

Clearly, any unevenness found on the path is imputable to the man or woman involved. But the teaching method the good God uses is able to adapt itself to this unevenness and turn it to man's benefit. Humility is called for here. And there is no need for man to concern himself with where exactly he is on the path of prayer: he is better employed trying to concentrate his worries on being generous with God. The fact is that a person who is sincerely seeking God is more concerned about the progress he is making in Love than his progress in prayer.

In the life of prayer, when someone is generous with God, the point will come when he finds it practically impossible to go back to meditation. Not because he has reached a fixed point of fervent prayer. On the contrary, it can happen that his sense of God's absence is so strong that it seems as the sole reality. When this happens, books provide no help and reverting to meditation becomes impossible. God seems to have become permanently silent. We are in the Nights that Saint John of the Cross spoke of —nights of terrible darkness, yet which presage the dawn of the new day in the spiritual journey.

The changeover from meditation to contemplation depends on God, as does everything that happens in the supernatural life. But it also depends on man's response to grace. The work of prayer is entirely God's, but that does not prevent man's actions from being genuinely meritorious: *God is at work in you, both to will and to work for his good pleasure.*[2] God is doing the work, but He brings about in man a will and a work that are truly human: because man

---

[2]Phil 2:13.

is fully free in willing and acting, his will and his action can be said to be truly his. That is why Saint Augustine said: *Try not to listen in vain. "Let us rejoice in God, who is our help (Ps 80:2)." For, if you were to do everything on your own, you would be in no need of a helper. Besides, if it were the case that nothing you did came from your own will, he would not be called a helper; for a helper is someone who helps a person to do something.*[3] We can say, then, once again, that progress in prayer depends on progress in imitating our Lord. The more, the better, a man lives according to the Spirit of our Lord, the more he will understand the language that Spirit uses, and the deeper he will enter the mystery of the trinitarian dialogue (1 Cor 2:14; Rom 8:5; 1 Cor 2:12).

For man, the step from meditation to contemplation means moving from a human to a divine way of doing things. Or better: moving from human action, elevated by grace, to superhuman action, also elevated by grace. It is at this point that the gifts of the Holy Spirit begin to act on the soul of the person who prays. And ordinary human language becomes quite inadequate; one has to give up using it: it is a resource which is no longer able to express what God and man want to tell each other: like the larva which has become a butterfly; it leaves the cocoon, which is of no use to it any longer, and flies away. We are already on the shores of contemplation.

This progress cannot occur unless one is humble. This humility will be seen, for example, in a person's readiness to be guided by a skilled teacher of the spiritual life, so as to avoid the danger which Ecclesiastes warned against: *woe to the man who is alone; for if he fall, he will have no one to lift him up.*[4] Humility also demands that he who prays should go back to using a book as often as need be, and

---

[3] *Enarrationes in Ps*, 143, 6.

[4] Eccles 4:10.

a book will be needed as often as it proves useful. One should not confuse inability to reflect, that is a feature of all true contemplation, with a laziness which flees from the effort which prayer always calls for.

We have already said that the Bible is the best of all meditation books. But it may not be good for a beginner to start by meditating on the Bible on his own, without any guidance. Above all, because there is no guarantee of individual inspiration by the Holy Spirit, for only the Church as such is guaranteed to be right in interpreting Scripture. And, also, because God usually acts through ordinary channels. We need, therefore, to avail ourselves of good books and good teachers, who will place in our hands the treasure of interpretations on the revealed word which the Church has built up over twenty centuries —the Church, our Mother and Teacher of the truth, enlightened by the Holy Spirit. That is why Saint Peter said: *You will do well to pay attention to the prophetic word as to a lamp shining in a dark place, until the day dawns and the morning star rises in your hearts. First of all, you must understand that no prophecy of scripture is a matter of one's own interpretation.*[5] And a little further on he adds: *Count the forbearance of our Lord as salvation. So also our beloved brother Paul wrote to you according to the wisdom given him, speaking of this as he does in all his letters. There are some things in them hard to understand, which the ignorant and unstable twist to their own destruction.*[6] The fruit of prayer which uses Scripture as its base often depends on having good teachers.

Holy Scripture needs to be properly understood. It contains teachings concerning things which affect all men in all eras; and

---

[5] 2 Pet 1: 19–20.
[6] 2 Pet 3: 15–16.

therefore they are relevant today too. To know what Scripture is really saying, one needs a certain familiarity with exegesis consistent with the Magisterium of the Church and one's own particular capacity. It is quite correct to say that the True Teacher is the Holy Spirit, but one should not undervalue the ordinary channels through which the Spirit acts too. In addition to this, one also needs to be familiar with the problems of the world one lives in so as to apply to them the answers the revealed word provides.

In saying that, we do not mean to imply that ordinary people should not be encouraged to read and meditate on the Bible. The Vatican II Constitution *Dei Verbum* recommends quite the opposite. But these are things pastors of souls need to take into account, especially those whose responsibility it is to initiate people into the life of prayer.

It is quite common nowadays for Holy Scripture to be left to one side, both in preaching and as far as prayer is concerned. With the sort of sociologizing and political preaching, with its meager or even non–existent supernatural content that is becoming so widespread, the Word of God is being used less and less. The same happens when preaching is confined to reading or commenting on *documents*, those documents which endlessly pour out of certain ecclesiastical office–laboratories, documents which are quite out of touch with reality and have very little supernatural content. As far as the practice of prayer is concerned, it is not unusual for the sacred books to be set aside in favour of other *pious* books, whose content may be more or less good but which can never take the place of Holy Scripture as an aid to prayer.

Nowadays, many factors militate against assimilating the Word of God as the Church understands it and passing it on to others (in a wide range of ways). As regards how the Word of God is expounded, in times gone by there was a much–criticized phenomenon which came to be called disincarnated spirituality. This was a style of preaching that was quite at odds with what God desired, because oratory tended to take the place of doctrine. They even used to talk of *sacred oratory* —a suspect term in itself because it was so big on oratory and so short on sacred. Pastors failed to offer the Christian people the Word of God in the form the Letter to the Hebrews describes it: as something living, effective, and always up to date.

But today the dangers have not disappeared, and disincarnation is still to be found in catechesis, but in new ways and new forms. Quite often theology uses excessively unintelligible jargon which many people think is scholarly; this would not matter so much if it were confined to the academic world, and were it not for the fact that this esoteric terminology is often used to cloak teachings or philosophies which are incompatible with the faith. The problem is that this jargon is often found in very basic oral and written cat- echesis, obscuring the content of the faith if not actually betraying it. Due to this, the ordinary Christian people, to whom these ques- tions and this sort of language are quite foreign, are being subjected to a new kind of disincarnation, which in some way is worse than earlier types. The apostle Saint Paul in fact warned the Corinthians about all this: *So with yourselves; if you in a tongue utter speech that is not intelligible, how will anyone know what is said? For you will be speaking into the air... If I do not know the meaning of the language, I shall be a foreigner to the speaker, and the speaker a foreigner to me... I thank God that I speak in tongues more than you all; nevertheless, in church I would rather speak five words with my mind, in order to instruct others, than ten thousand words in a tongue.*[7] Preaching the Word of God is also threatened today by the danger of secularism. It is not uncommon for preaching to concentrate on expounding temporal options having to do with political matters: lessons are drawn from Revelation in such a suspect way that it is difficult not to think the word of God is being intentionally prostituted (Jer 23:36; 2 Cor 4:2; Rev 22: 18–19).

It must be remembered that anyone who wants to initiate others into the life of prayer, revealing to them the inexhaustible riches of the Word of God, simply cannot do so unless he has genuine love for God and men. For it is impossible to understand Scripture, or help others understand it, if oneself does not possess the Spirit of God, Who is essentially Love.

---

[7]1 Cor 14: 9.11.18–19.

PRAYER AND PURIFICATION

We said earlier that advancement in the life of prayer involves a purification process too. Being introduced into the life of God and in the dialogue of the Trinity means becoming intimate with God, and for this to happen man needs to let himself be led by the Spirit of Jesus (Rom 8:14). Progress in prayer is progress in friendship and love between God and man, and that is impossible unless man first undergoes purification. Saint John of the Cross explains this well in his *Ascent*, in his teaching about the *Nights*. This purification which man needs to undergo is but spiritual poverty, detachment from things, and mortification of one's passions (Mt 5:3; 10:38; 16:24; Mk 8:34).

But prayer itself is also a means of purification. One has hardly begun to pray than one already needs to make an effort to persevere at it. The book of the Acts uses this very word *persevere* when it says that the group of the first disciples persevered all the time in the practice of prayer (Acts 1:14; cf. 2:42). However, we are not referring to that here: we mean the much deeper purification which takes place at the higher levels of prayer. At these levels God purifies those He calls to be intimate with Him, in a way that those who have not experienced it personally cannot imagine. For, those whom the Spirit has brought into the Son, in order to lead them to the Father, must needs participate in the cross of the Son made man (Rom 6:4; 2 Cor 4:11) in such a way that the more intense that participation is the more intimate will their sharing in the divine life be. So, there is a purification necessary for the life of prayer —and also a purification which takes place in prayer and through prayer. Both kinds of purification are a consequence of a Christian's need to share in the cross of Jesus Christ, for his own benefit and that of others, because he forms part of the supernatural organism of the Mystical Body of Christ: *Now I rejoice in my sufferings for your sake, and in my flesh I complete what is lacking in Christ's afflictions for the sake of his body, that is, the church.*[1] Sharing in our Lord's passion is something which takes place in all the events of a Christian's life, but it happens in a very special way in prayer, all the more so as one advances therein.

---

[1]Col 1:24.

DISTRACTIONS AS AN ELEMENT OF PURIFICATION

A very basic type of purification of prayer —far removed from real purifications, which come later— is the struggle one needs to keep up against distractions which get in the way. Distractions are something a person who prays can expect for quite a while —at least that is normally the case— and he cannot know whether in fact they will ever disappear entirely. Once the fervor and special helps that are a feature of the very early stages of prayer disappear, distractions are bound to come.

In mystical theology it is often said that the spiritual life is a path one has to travel along: a journey of the soul towards God, as Saint Bonaventure put it; or a series of dwellings or stages one has to pass through before one reaches the interior of the castle, according

to Saint Teresa; or a long ascent which leads to the summit of the
mount of perfection, according to Saint John of the Cross; or a series
of ages one has to pass through as the interior life develops, according
to Garrigou–Lagrange. All the writers on this subject agree that
there is this road one must travel on. A road which has a beginning,
certain equipment given to the person traveling on it, difficulties to
be met, progress to be made, and, eventually, an end. Everything
is easy to start with, but difficulties are not slow to appear. The
mystics have written much doctrine to teach about this subject and
they offer various arguments by way of explanation. They say, for
example, that God wants to purify man of his selfishness and to
prevent him from seeking himself; hence the loss of sensible fervor.
And distractions are, perhaps, the first difficulties to appear in the
life of prayer.

The first thing one has to do about distractions in prayer is
not be surprised or shocked by them; then one has to deal with
them patiently and humbly. Purification of the memory and of the
imagination takes a long time, and in the course of this one should
remember that it is not a matter of suppressing these faculties: they
are very necessary for prayer; quietism was condemned a long time
ago.[1]

Distractions in prayer may be a person's own fault: they may
derive from sin or lukewarmness or sheer human weakness. Distractions of this sort can destroy one's prayer life, so one needs to make
a special effort to deal with them. The remedies are the same as
apply in the struggle against lukewarmness: particularly, good spiritual direction, mortification (especially interior mortification) and

---

[1]DS 2201–2269. Quietism is a complex phenomenon which in its classic form is
found in the 17th century, but its roots go back to the Gnostic heresies. Basically
quietism says that the soul's faculties need to be suppressed (with resultant loss of
one's personality) in order to become united to God. See also DS 2365–2368.

a sincere desire to do one's prayer well. We already pointed out that prayer calls for a certain remote preparation, which means an asceticism applying to the faculties of the soul, and constant practice of the presence of God.

However, the most common distractions in prayer are the involuntary ones, assuming that the person praying has good will. Certainly the most practical thing we can say about distractions of this sort is that one has to bear with them, patiently and humbly, for as long as they last. We have already said that difficulties in prayer are part of the teaching method God uses: His aim is to get man to stop seeking himself and to love God in a purer, more disinterested way. These difficulties increase our humility and our trust in God, and they help a person to know himself better and to realize that his own efforts, alone, will get him nowhere.

The struggle against involuntary distractions needs to be a vigorous one —but one must at all costs stay serene. God does not take distractions away as long as they are needed. On the path of the spiritual life distractions can be a means of purification and a special way of sharing in our Lord's cross. Saint Teresa came to the conclusion that at times it was not even a good idea to fight with one's imagination, this madwoman of the house, as she described it. She thought it was better just to ignore it, provided one's mind and heart are united to God. Distractions of this sort can often be turned into prayer by fighting against them and making a prayer of petition about their content. Anyway, even if one puts up a good fight, one should not forget that prayer is not meant to be torture for the soul, because, in the last analysis, it is a conversation with and a loving outpouring to a Person Whom one loves. Prayer is frequently a cause of suffering, even very intense suffering, because it is the ideal place for sharing in some way in the passion and death of the Loved One; but the suffering that prayer involves never has anything to do with psychological pain.

At an early stage in contemplation a point comes when the use of words and of the imagination becomes futile and even impossible. When that happens, it is better to allow heart and mind to rest tranquilly in the Lord: *In praying do not heap up words, as the Gentiles do; for they think that they will be heard for their many words.*[2]

---

[2]Mt 6:7.

TEMPTATIONS AS AN ELEMENT OF PURIFICATION

The most serious distractions one can suffer in prayer are temptations; prayer is no stranger to temptation, even very severe temptation. There is nothing surprising about this because man has to put up a greater fight the nearer he gets to God, and prayer is the ideal place for this approach to God to occur. The devil normally piles on difficulties at this stage, but these difficulties actually help the person who prays to share more fully in Christ's passion. The Gospel tells us that our Lord went out into the desert to pray and do penance and *be tempted by the devil*;[1] from this one can deduce that certain times, allocated specially for prayer, can be times when temptations noticeably increase. We can see this even more clearly

---

[1] Mt 4:1; Mk 1:13; Lk 4: 1–2.

in the Gospel episode of the agony in the garden, where our Lord
was assaulted by a desire to avoid suffering and by an anguish which
went so far as to make Him sweat blood. One thing is certain: anyone who wishes to give himself fully to a life of prayer must be ready
to undergo severe tests and great suffering.

One of the most common temptations in the life of prayer is
the temptation to give up prayer. To give up prayer and even the
spiritual life. But the fact is that all sorts of temptations can occur in
prayer: from that of pride to that of spiritual gluttony, lust, and even
the temptation to despair; the list could be extended indefinitely.[2]

If borne patiently, temptations for which one is not responsible
are not an obstacle to prayer. A person who prays should not become
sad because of such temptations or desist from praying, even if his
suffering is very great. These temptations are like storms at sea:
the water becomes rough on the surface but deep down all is calm.
The soul can experience here very acute suffering and, at the very
same time, a serene peace deep down. Temptation, perhaps very
painful temptation which causes moral and even physical suffering,
is changed in this context into something incredibly beautiful. This
kind of temptation can also seem to last for a very short time, despite
the acuteness of suffering, because one's sense of time during prayer
can sometimes be quite deceptive: in the course of prayer man's
faculties can be raised to act in a supernatural and superhuman

---

[2]Saint Peter of Alcántara, in his *Tratado de la oración y meditación* discusses
temptations in prayer. As regards temptations to impurity, which he calls *inop-
portune thoughts*, he deals with them expressly in Part 2, Chap. 4, 5th warning,
where he says: *The remedy is to fight manfully and perseveringly, although the re-
sistance one puts up should not be very fatiguing or draining for the spirit, because
this business is not so much a matter of effort as of grace and humility.* In the
6th warning he provides useful and very sensible advice about how to deal with
sleepiness in prayer; which is remarkable in a man like him, who lived such an
ascetical life.

way, through very intimate participation in the divine life, giving man even a mysterious sense of time.

A person who prays can sometimes be tempted by the idea that he has been wasting his time, or he can feel that his prayer is displeasing to God. This sort of thing is simply a temptation, and the person should be content in the knowledge that he has acted with good will. Ordinarily God's plans do not include making known to us, while we are in this world, the fruit our labor bears —or even whether it bears any fruit. For our part it should suffice to plant and water, leaving it to God to look after the growth (1 Cor 3:7). Besides, uncertainty of this type leads man to practice hope and trust in God (these do give him a sense of security, though by another route), and it causes him to experience, here too, participation in our Lord's passion.

PRAYER AND THE CROSS

The hour of darkness in prayer is the hour of the Nights, and a person who prays has to be ready to experience those nights and to persevere. This is the time for him to meet God in suffering, just as earlier he met him in consolation: *It is right to declare thy steadfast love in the morning, and thy faithfulness by night.*[1] At all times God should be blessed —when things are easy and when they are difficult: in the daytime, when one can see clearly, we sing of the goodness and mercy of God; then, during the night of difficulty, we need to keep a hold on God's truth, sure and confident that He is with us. At these points in a person's life, when all is dark, it can seem that he has achieved nothing: *Master, we toiled all night and*

---

[1]Ps 92:3.

took nothing.[2] Moments of this sort occur quite often in a life, such as that of a Christian, in which prayer is an important part. But it is also true that that night of the spirit, when everything seems to be going wrong, is the point for asserting one's hope in God, holding fast to His truth, and saying with Saint Peter: *But at your word I will let down the nets.* The psalmist describes as blessed the man whose delight, day and night, is in the law of God (Ps 1:2). Therefore, in the dark night of prayer, one needs to ask for the gift of perseverance.

Christian prayer does not exclude suffering. For, since prayer is a point where those in love draw closer to one another, it is logical that the lover should get to where the loved one is, to share his life and therefore his sufferings. Saint Luke speaks to us about our Lord's prayer in the night of Gethsemane: *Being in an agony... his sweat became like great drops of blood.*[3] And the Letter to the Hebrews says that Jesus *offered up prayers and supplications, with loud cries and tears, to him who was able to save him from death, and he was heard for his godly fear.*[4] Christian prayer is not always pleasant, at least not in the ordinary sense of that word. It certainly excludes sadness (Jas 5:13; cf. 1 Thess 5: 16–17; Jn 3:29), but never suffering. For sadness or gloominess is the opposite of joy, which is such a special feature of Christian living (Phil 4:4; 1 Thess 5:16; 2 Cor 6:10), whereas, on the contrary, our Lord linked suffering to a beatitude that begins in this world (Mt 5:4).

Those midnight moments of life —the middle of the night or the darkest time of night, as Saint John of the Cross called it— are the times when prayer is most necessary, precisely because they

---

[2] Lk 5:5.

[3] Lk 22:44.

[4] Heb 5:7.

are the difficult times. And they are the moments when we can be
most confident that we will be listened to, as our Lord Himself says
in a parable about prayer, the parable of the importunate friend:
*Which of you who has a friend will go to him at midnight and say to
him...*[5] And the friend the parable speaks of, who came at midnight,
was listened to. The Bridegroom in the parable of the ten virgins
also comes at midnight, at the darkest time of night, therefore, and
when he is least expected: *At midnight there was a cry: Behold,
the bridegroom! Come out to meet him.*[6] All this actually happens
in prayer: the Lord usually comes in the midnight of prayer, at the
time of suffering, after testing and purifying the fidelity and patience
of the saints, thereby completing the work of the redemption of the
world. Hence the need to be on the watch and to persevere, hoping
against hope (Rom 4:18), confident that the Lord will come at any
time —always at a time one never foresees— and confident, too,
that His fidelity will not fail: *Watch, therefore —for you do not
know when the master of the house will come, in the evening, or at
midnight, or at cockcrow, or in the morning.*[7]

As we have said, the suffering one experiences in the life of prayer
is caused both by the person's need to be purified and by his need
to share in the Lord's mission. These two kinds of purification become one. But, whereas purification from one's own sins can come
to an end —through attaining, with the help of grace, a state in
which purification is no longer necessary— that does not apply as
regards purification for the sins of others. That is why, although
purification of the senses and potentialities of the soul can be attained (and the *Nights* corresponding to that purification be a thing

---

[5]Lk 11:5.

[6]Mt 25:6.

[7]Mk 13:35.

of the past), sufferings during prayer will last one's whole life long. But the sufferings proper to this second stage have features which differentiate them from the earlier, purgative stage. The suffering destined to give one a share in our Lord's passion for the sins of men, even though it may be more intense, is always accompanied by joy, serenity, fortitude, patience, hope, and, in general, the fruits which the presence of the Spirit causes in a person who loves God and which are here found in great profusion. However, the two types of suffering are not found in exact continuity: they can occur mixed together (timewise), and sometimes one will predominate, sometimes the other. But it is certain that, when the *Nights* are already something in the past, the suffering one now experiences is so different from the earlier one that one can say it has turned into joy, which is why the Bridegroom can say to the bride in the Song of Songs:

> *Arise, my love,*
> *my fair one, and come away;*
> *for lo, the winter is past,*
> *the rain is over and gone.*
> *The flowers appear on the earth,*
> *the time of singing has come,*
> *and the voice of the turtledove*
> *is heard in our land.*[8]

The Bridegroom comes when winter is past and the rains are over, for no one ever encounters Him without first suffering, since love always tends to have a share in the life of the loved one: *'Tell me, foolish one, where does the greatest degree of similitude and comparison lie?' He answered, 'Between the Friend and the Beloved.'*

---

[8]Sg 2: 10–12.

They asked him why this was so, and he said that it was due to the love they had for one another.[9]

Sufferings and trials should not prevent us from persevering. Only those who keep going will come to know what prayer is. Scripture delights in promising to these the prize that awaits perseverance: *He who conquers and who keeps my works until the end... I will give him the morning star.*[10] Once again we find a reference to the morning, to that point at dawn when the daystar appears, marking the beginning of a new day. The morning star which is given to those who persevere isJesus, the Star which those who keep advancing on the paths of prayer feel to be the best possible prize: *I, Jesus..., I am the root and offspring of David, the bright morning star.*[11]

---

[9]Ramon Lull, *Libro del Amigo y del Amado*, 191.

[10]Rev 2: 26–28.

[11]Rev 22:16.

BASIC IDEAS ABOUT CONTEMPLATION

The first question that might be asked here is whether this subject is relevant nowadays. The answer is a very definite yes. A world which is experiencing suffering and which hungers for God, even if it does not admit the latter, needs to speak to God and to listen to Him. The moment may come, if it realizes that its present course is leading to madness, when it may once more feel the need for prayer. The Church also has to realize that it cannot make progress unless it prays and that its very existence depends on it (Lk 21:36; Mt 26:41). To speak of prayer, and of prayer as practiced by the saints, is to speak of the only reliable means available to us to keep on the right path. Believing in prayer means believing in the goodness of God, Who has shown Himself to be so generous towards man. And it also means believing in man, at least in many men and

women who refuse to renounce their friendship with God and their
conversation with Him. To speak of contemplation means believing
that holiness is not a thing of the past; it is nothing other than the
happy conjunction of God's goodness and man's generous response.
It is true that many people, even ecclesiastics, are ashamed these
days to talk about holiness. But that says nothing against holiness;
a dawn or a sunset does not cease to be beautiful even if people are
bent on saying it is ugly.

By contemplation we mean, here, the more advanced degrees of
mental prayer, which man cannot attain unless he is led by special
graces from God. These special graces involve, on man's part, a special kind of co–operation, which takes the form of a high degree of
generosity whereby he responds to the grace which attracts him and
raises him up. Contemplation is an intimate and special, supernatural and superhuman, type of communication between God and man.
Supernatural because it presupposes sanctifying grace; and superhuman because in it the gifts of the Holy Spirit are brought into being
in a special way, thereby raising man to a state where his normal
mode of knowing and loving is greatly exceeded. The infused virtues
which sanctifying grace brings with itself are set in motion by actual
graces, in such a way that man acts supernaturally, so that he is enabled to do things that exceed his natural capacity; but this occurs
in a human mode and in keeping with man's normal psychological
make–up. However, the special graces that contemplation causes in
man make him work in a superhuman mode, enabling him to know
and to love in the divine mode. Contemplation is a very special development of the divine life in man, resulting from a union of divine
and human generosities. This union is made possible by grace; but
certainly, and for that very reason, man's activity here is a truly

human action and is therefore meritorious.[1] When speaking of con-templation, one has to use terminology —singular, special graces; special gifts of the Holy Spirit; elevated degrees of prayer...— which might suggest that contemplation, in the last analysis, is equivalent to what are usually termed extraordinary phenomena of the mystical life; that could lead one to lose sight of the essence of contemplative life. Extraordinary mystical phenomena, although they can occur at certain elevated degrees of prayer, are not the essence of contempla-tion. Obviously, genuine contemplation presupposes an interior life beyond what is normal; but one needs to choose one's words care-fully, because extraordinary phenomena can fail to occur in lives that are genuinely contemplative. There is also a genuine type of mystical life which is undetected even by the person who experiences it. The truth is that genuine contemplative prayer shuns publicity: even the person himself may be unaware, if not unaware that it is happening, at least unaware in the sense that he does not correctly interpret the facts as being mystical facts. Contemplative prayer is extraordinary, but it is not always spectacular. The Virgin Mary, for example, who is the true teacher of contemplative prayer for the whole Church, could not have lived a more extraordinary life and yet hers was not a spectacular life. Spectacular gifts and charisms are things God gives when He so chooses, and then the sheer scale and marvel of them becomes quite patent. In the true saint, the presence of God becomes in some way tangible, and through it we become aware that we are seeing a glimpse of eternal life. But we should not confuse accessories with the main thing. And the main

---

[1] We have said that we are leaving to one side the various technical questions which arise in connection with contemplation. Here we are speaking, simply, of that elevated degree of prayer at which God gives those who love Him access to His more intimate life while they are still in this world; and the person concerned is in some way aware of being on that higher plane. For us, contemplation is, then, a singular grace but one which God is ready to grant to those who desire it.

thing, here as always, is charity. Saint Paul, speaking about gifts and charisms, and after listing them, adds that *I will show you a still more excellent way*;[2] and then be begins to speak about charity (1 Cor 13), going on to warn of the dangers that certain extraordinary phenomena such as tongues and prophecy can lead to (1 Cor 14). An act of charity is no less admirable than a vision or the gift of tongues, and it has the great advantage that charity never deceives. The acts of charity, great or small, which might run right through an entire life, can take all kinds of forms, not unconnected with humility, simplicity, or unselfconscious beauty. It is quite likely that the true saint never knows he is one until God lets him see it when he is on the threshold of eternity. The gift of tongues, for example, is a wonderful thing, but it is no more admirable than the ability to understand well what God has communicated to men through His Word, and being able to pass it on. And yet the great gift of being able to preach the Gospel to others at one's particular time in history is very rare, though not spectacular; and it is a gift God does not give unless there is a true life of prayer which lets itself be led by the motions of the Spirit. There is no doubt but that this gift —of preaching the Gospel— is of much more benefit to the Church than the gift of tongues (1 Cor 14:19). The Church can survive without the gift of tongues, but not without the gift of preaching: it is an absolute necessity for her (1 Cor 9:16). In fact the shortage of this gift is one of the symptoms of the grave crisis the Church is experiencing at the present time, because, although there is a proliferation everywhere of *charismatics* of every type and description, there is a great scarcity of good, simple preachers of the Gospel to spread the truth of God's Word throughout the world.

---

[2] 1 Cor 12:31.

ON THE PATHS OF CONTEMPLATION

The grace of contemplation is the high point of the work of God in man. A grace that brings with it two things: the sheer fact of divine–human intimacy, which is the masterpiece of divine craftsmanship; and man's generosity, or his affirmative response to God's overtures. Thus, contemplation is, at the same time, the great triumph of both God and man. Contemplation is for man the greatest of all graces, because man knows that in this grace he receives the Love of God itself. Or better still: God is offering Himself to man in the form of Gift. The Holy Spirit is the Gift par excellence. Contemplation brings about, fully, the elevation of man, from his natural state to the state of intimate friendship with God: *No longer do I call you servants... but I call you friends.*[1] In

---

[1]Jn 15:15.

contemplation man experiences, in a very intense way, the Love of God. And he perceives it as love, as something entirely free and gratuitous: love as the pure gift of Love. The gift of a Love Which desires nothing; the only thing It can do is love and give love, which means give Itself (as such Love), holding nothing back. Man at last comes to see that without Love there is no love, and that life devoid of Love would be empty and meaningless.

> *Who is coming up from the wilderness,*
> *leaning upon her beloved?*[2]

The bride has reached this point leaning on the Beloved and being led by Him. The Beloved's Love produces intense love in her which now makes her see that everything that went before was a desert, as it were: *He who does not love remains in death.*[3]

But contemplation is a singular grace whereby God reveals His Love, not only to the contemplative, but also to others. Contemplation leads to holiness, and holiness in man is a form of epiphany in which the divine is made manifest. Behind the saint, but manifesting Himself through him, stands God. The Baptist spoke of One wWho would come after him, and Whom he had to reveal (Jn 1: 30–31), while our Lord sent His disciples ahead of Him (Lk 10:1) to those places He planned to visit. The saint, or the contemplative, or the man who takes the Love of God seriously, has to be out in front, so that behind him or through him God can be seen. This is the true meaning of Christian witness: to let the world see Jesus through us. Strictly speaking, people do not hold the saint in admiration or

---

[2]Sg 8:5.

[3]1 Jn 3:14.

love him: they admire and love what they discover from his presence; that is why it is easy for the saint to be humble. The saint as epiphany or witness shows that holiness consists more in self–deprivation than in acquisition. The saint deprives himself so that God may be seen through him. Therefore holiness is within the reach of all. If it consisted in attainment and achievement, it would be impossible: it would mean obtaining things which are far beyond our reach; on the other hand, who cannot get rid of the few rags he is clad in? The contemplative has discovered that it is not a matter of climbing up but of going down, and that achievements are not as important as becoming children (Mt 18:3). It could not be otherwise, once God became a child and showed us the way. The halo of the saint is really something transparent, and through it one is able to see God. Simple people expressed this in their own way by painting the saint surrounded by a very special light, but really they were right. The Latin word *clarificare* also means to glorify; clarifying and glorifying thus became synonymous; that is very appropriate because the saint is charity, transparency, simplicity, childlikeness. The characteristics found in saints are those proper to children, which is why it is to children that the Kingdom of heaven is promised (Mt 18:4). Thus the glory of the saints is really their clarity, truth, and transparency, through which one is able to see the glory of God.

That is why the saint, or the contemplative if you wish, practices total self–deprivation (Mk 10:21). Otherwise there is neither transparency nor, consequently, any witnessing. The saint is, in the eyes of others, the man whose only possession is God: *Carry no purse, no bag, no sandals.*[4] That is the point when their witness moves the hearts of men, by exposing to them the deceitfulness of the world

---

[4]Lk 10:4.

they live in. For this reason the devil cannot but hate the saint.
By revealing Christ through the transparency of his life, the saint
also reveals all truth —for that is precisely what Christ is: *I am the
truth.*[5] And this exposes the entire structure of deceit that the devil
and the world have jointly built: the injustice, the cowardice, the
opportunism, and the idolatry of the age: *I saw a beast rising out of
the sea, with ten horns and seven heads, with ten diadems upon its
horns and a blasphemous name upon its heads. And the beast that
I saw was like a leopard, its feet were like a bear's, and its mouth
was like a lion's mouth. And to it the dragon gave his power and
his throne and great authority. One of its heads seemed to have a
mortal wound, but its mortal wound was healed, and the whole earth
followed the beast with wonder. Men worshipped the dragon, for he
had given his authority to the beast, and they worshipped the beast,
saying, "Who is like the beast, and who can fight against it?"*[6] Everyone pays obeisance to the beast: Christians and non–Christians,
lay people and clergy, old and young, intellectuals and workers, in
a desperate effort to hold on somehow to some sort of existence and
stay on the side of the Powers of this world. The beast will never
forgive those who oppose him (Rev 13: 15–17), and that is the real
reason behind the campaigns waged against those who refuse to accept the System, against those who strive to hold on to their sense
of the supernatural —in other words, against those who hold on to
their belief that religion is what unites or links (*religere*) man to
God. In a world that has become phallocentric, priestly celibacy
practiced out of love for the Kingdom of heaven, for example, is a
scandal and a living rejection of the pansexualist and Freudian view
of man: a proof of the victory of the Spirit over the flesh. But, in the

---

[5] Jn 14:6.

[6] Rev 13: 1–4.

last analysis, what is at issue here is something much more serious. What is at issue here is whether it is or is not possible to love God more than created things. Celibacy is a proof that it is possible, and that is why it is treated as an enemy; all the other arguments put forward to justify its abolition are a mere excuse.

* * *

We have already said that contemplative prayer has often been regarded as a situation where man has largely a passive role. In this prayer man is flooded by God's light, since it is God Who takes the initiative here, in such a way that the soul contemplates and receives; it has advanced far from the time when it had to make the effort of discursive reasoning demanded by simple meditation.

Now, prayer is an outpouring of love, and love is reciprocity. This is even more the case the more perfect love is, as it happens in contemplative prayer. Man is never more man than when his *I* is pronounced as a *thou* by the lips of God. Since contemplative prayer is a transfusion, an interflowing, of lives, it cannot be correct to describe it as passivity (or mere receptivity) on the part of one of the lovers: *I came that they may have life, and have it abundantly.*[7] And Saint Paul said: *Then I shall understand fully, even*

---

[7] Jn 10:10.

as I have been fully understood.[8] If prayer is an outpouring of love, and contemplative prayer is the most perfect form of prayer, it cannot consist in mere passivity, or even a situation where passivity is predominant in either of the lovers. On the contrary, since contemplation is perfect love, the most perfect that can occur in this life, it must contain at one and the same time passivity and activity —and that on the part of both lovers. Contemplative love, as we have also pointed out earlier, is a faithful copy of the life of the Trinity, in which the Father and the Son together spirate the Holy Spirit, Who is, thus, both a giving and a surrender. The loving effusion is, indeed, passivity, insofar as in it the loved one is entirely received; but it is also, to an equal degree, activity or giving, insofar as there is in it a total surrender to the beloved. With the result that the beloved is also the lover, and the lover is also the loved one:

I am my beloved's, and my beloved is mine.[9]

Contemplative prayer is as active as it is passive, and this applies both to God and to man. The human *I* is never more identical with himself, in his being that very *I*, than when he is addressed as *thou* —most familiarly— by the divine I. Man truly finds himself when he loses his own life for the love of God (Mk 8:35; Lk 9:24). The total self–surrender that man makes, with the help of grace, in contemplative prayer can never be described as passivity. In this prayer man is *known*, but he also is *knowing*. Contemplation is for man a superabundance of life, because in the transfusion of lives that takes place there, Christ hHimself, Who is Life (Jn 14:6; 1:4), lives one and the same life as the contemplative (Gal 2:20; Col 3:4). Now,

---

[8]1 Cor 13:12.
[9]Sg 6:3.

receiving Jesus' life as our own requires, at the same time, giving our life so that it may be His. In love, one receives everything at the same time as one gives everything. Therefore it is impossible for contemplation to exist if one has not lost (given) one's life for the Lord: *He who loses his life for my sake...* We need to remember that the idea of *losing* one's own life, for His sake, means much more than a superficial view of things would suggest. It refers not simply to the fact of accepting death when it comes; nor (though it includes it) does it refer just to the desire to offer one's life to God in a supreme act of martyrdom: the martyr offers his life to God because he would rather lose it than cease to love Him above all things; but the martyr gives his life when faced with death, whereas here we are referring to giving one's life in the face of life; or, to put it better: here it is a matter of giving up living what would have been one's own life, at the very time when one had full scope to 'do one's own thing.' Losing one's life, taken in this sense, means accepting to a large extent the interpretation that one's life has been wasted (this is an interpretation not illuminated by faith) or has not been put to good use, in the same sense as when we say, for example, that we have wasted time. In this way, looking at things the way the world does, our life can be a waste, a complete failure compared with what we could have achieved (Wis 5:4). And yet, by accepting this *waste*, man accepts nothing less than God's scale of values, which is totally different from his own. Man *spoils* his life, closing it off to human possibilities, rendering it *useless* to other people, but doing so under the guidance of faith, giving it a sacrificial meaning. But, in fact, that is the truest and best of sacrifices. Since the coming of Christ, sacrifices of animals and scapegoats (Heb 10:5) are no longer acceptable; on the contrary, the Christian, who now shares in Christ's priesthood, is also, like Him, priest and victim at the same time, and able therefore to offer his own life as a sacrifice. If the words of the Gospel are not empty words, then losing one's life means being ready to accept human failure, failure to accomplish all the achievements one could have, even apparently supernatural goals (that was the situation of Christ on the Cross) and, instead, putting oneself in God's hands, accepting Hhis ways. According to this, *losing* one's life does not imply undervaluing it, but rather realizing that only God is worthy of it.

* * *

Contemplation is the summit of God's masterpiece —divine–human friendship. It is the greatest of all graces, and therefore something man cannot explain: he cannot explain its essence or account for its existence. The bride knows that if she has reached this point it is because she owes everything to the Bridegroom; and so she says in the Song of Songs:

> *Who is this coming up from the wilderness,*
> *leaning upon her beloved?*
> *Under the apple tree I awakened you.*
> *There your mother was in travail with you,*
> *there she who bore you was in travail.*[10]

---

[10]Sg 8:5.

The bride, as we have said, has to come up from the desert leaning upon her Beloved. The desert is her earlier situation, where she was without the Beloved, and which she ardently desires to leave. But to recognize the desert for what it is, a desert, one needs first to know the Beloved. For someone who has chosen not to know the Love of God, the worst punishment is not recognizing, either, the desert of one's own heart: *He who does not love remains in death.*[11] In addition, the bride feels herself lifted out of her sins. It is on the rough canvas of her wretchedness that God weaves the precious fabric of their mutual friendship:

> *Under the apple tree I awakened you.*
> *There your mother was in travail with you,*
> *there she who bore you was in travail.*

Human shortcomings are no obstacle to the contemplative life. On the contrary: for it is precisely by using those shortcomings as if they were withered leaves that God sets alight the bonfire of divine–human love. A bonfire that finds plenty of fuel in man's awareness of what God has made of his wretchedness: How can one love if one has not received something? The Son, indeed, loves the Father because He knows that He has received everything from Him.[12] But man knows that he has been created, and then begotten or re–created

---

[11]1 Jn 3:14.

[12]When the Son is said to have received everything from the Father, that is not meant to be understood as some sort of creation; it refers to the communication of the divine essence to the Word by way of generation. Apropos of texts such as Jn 3:35; 5:20 and 17:24, Saint Thomas points out that the verb *to give* means an activity which originates in love, and therefore it cannot be used of the communication of the divine essence to the Word, since that communication is a generation which has its source in God's nature, not in His will. Cf. Saint Thomas Aquinas, *Super Evangelium S. Ioannis Lectura*, on Jn 3: 34–35. See also A. Feuillet's commentary in his *Le mystère de l'amour divin dans la Théologie johannique* (Paris, 1972), p. 40. Feuillet clarifies certain aspects of Saint Thomas' interpretation of these texts;

to a new life, and redeemed as well. The quoted passage from the
Song seems to refer to this. In fact, the saints always find, in their
awareness of their own sins (forgiven sins), abundant material to
burn in the love of God. All that is required of man is that he be
aware of this, in an attitude of humility and hope.

Contemplative prayer is, therefore, grace, a very special, unique
grace because it is so elevated. We have reached the threshold of
eternal life, where all is grace, as Bernanos' country priest says when
he is dying. Man can now let himself be drenched by the torrential
rain that falls from heaven; very distant now are those heavy chores,
so slow and exhausting, of getting the water from the well with the
help of the donkey, in Saint Teresa's famous example.

And, as we have said, it is also a superabundance of life. Thanks
to it, man while still in this world is able to know in a way that
he could never have known and to love in a way he could never
have loved. In contemplative life man is not despoiled of his own
nature; rather, that nature is raised up and enabled to achieve its
full potential; firstly on the natural level and then, going far beyond
that, on the supernatural level. Contemplative prayer is a divine–
human partnership in which man loses nothing and gains everything.
And because man thereby becomes more human than he ever was,
he also becomes freer and more responsible. In loving man God does
not annihilate man, but rather elevates him. Contemplation is the
affirmation of the dialogue of love, taking it as far as it can go, and
therefore it is also the full affirmation of the *I* and the *thou*.

The sovereignly active role of man in contemplation was, however, missed, neglected, by those doctrines which, though promoting

---

he says that they can refer only to the Word incarnate (because otherwise the Holy
Spirit would be the principle of generation of the Son, as said earlier). We, for our
part, will stay with Saint Thomas' interpretation.

the union of man with the divinity, argued that man's role is a passive one; these doctrines range from Stoic *apathia* to the quietisms of the seventeenth century, visiting en route the various forms of Manicheism and Gnosticism (found for example in the teachings of the Cathars, Beguins, and Begards). These doctrines insisted that man should be passive to allow the Spirit to act freely and the soul to be transformed into the Godhead and become, therefore, incapable of sinning: all that man needs to do then is to let himself be brought along, fully sure that everything done by him will be good. In this way he will be freed from sin, because if everything he does is under the influence of the Spirit, then sin cannot happen. One can detect at the base of this attitude a desire not to recognize the human *I*, especially the I as sinner; or the desire to excise the dialoguing *I* in his full personality and, therefore, as a being fully responsible for his actions. This approach does contain a desire to reach the Godhead, but by the easy way, avoiding the steep and narrow way of the cross; hence its rejection of asceticism, of rules, of virtues, or of the Church as institution.

Contemplation is a foretaste of eternal life to a very elevated degree. It is, then, a sort of first–fruits. Grace itself is that; but in the case of contemplation the veil is drawn aside in some way. Contemplation is vision and fruition of God to a very high degree, but still in the context of faith: *So faith, hope, love abide, these three;*[13] and the Apostle also says: *Our knowledge is imperfect and our prophecy is imperfect; but when the perfect comes, the imperfect will pass away.*[14] The vision of God that the Christian is given in contemplative prayer is always a vision of faith; it is not something we see through our bodily senses (Heb 11:1). Therefore it is imperfect:

---

[13]1 Cor 13:13.

[14]1 Cor 13: 9–10.

Now we see in a mirror dimly, but then face to face.[15] It is true, of course, that even our vision of God in eternal life is imperfect, in the original use of that word: it is incomplete, unfinished (Mt 11:27).[16] But contemplation is located halfway between the simple knowledge of God that a simple faith provides and the sort of knowledge of God that one obtains in Heaven. The contemplative is conscious of the great distance between what he sees and what he has yet to see, between what he possesses and what he will possess in the future. In no way has he attained his final goal, but what he already is experiencing is enough to give him some inkling of what that goal is really like. If he advances further on the path of contemplation he is given additional light, which shows him how far he has still to go and the infinite distance that separates the two extremes which are destined to meet. Saint Thomas and most medieval theologians spoke of an evening knowledge and a morning knowledge. We can also apply here that distinction to imperfect knowledge (faith) and to perfect knowledge (which will happen in heaven). Man cannot but yearn for perfect knowledge, perfect possession, of God. The bride in the Song looks eagerly for the Bridegroom; she wants to be with Him, to know Him, and to possess Him:

---

[15] 1 Cor 13:12.

[16] It is not *perfect* or finished in terms of the object contemplated, that is, God, Infinite Being; but it is complete in terms of man, in the sense that it will satisfy all his appetites.

When gentle dawn is not yet morning
and in the flushed valley, amid the hills,
the apple exhales its fragances
and in the distance the turtledove coos,
you call for your bride, your sister,
in ancient echoes of old songs.
The wind interrupts its moaning,
bringing your call to my ears.
I have crossed the brook through the ford,
and await with burning desire,
seated under a shady oak, to see if the beloved
decides to meet with me,
and if the news they brought from him
will last from night to morn.
And, while I await, by the yews
a flock of swifts flies low.[17]

---

[17]In the original:

Cuando el alba suave aún no es mañana
y en el valle florido, entre los cejos,
exhala sus fragancias la manzana
y se arrulla la tórtola a lo lejos,
tú clamas por tu esposa, por tu hermana,
con eco antiguo de cantares viejos.
Y el viento hace una pausa en sus gemidos
trayendo tu reclamo a mis oídos.
Cruzando ya el arroyo por el vado,
sentado aguardo bajo umbrosa encina
con ardorosas ansias, por si Amado
encontrarse conmigo determina,
y ver si su noticia que me han dado
de vesperal la hiciera matutina.
Y, mientras que yo espero, por los tejos
vuela baja una banda de vencejos.

The bride desires to know the Bridegroom, to know Him fully, by the clear light of morning. But, as we have always said, love is something mutual, and therefore the Bridegroom too cries out for the bride; He actively seeks her and passionately calls to her. The ancient echo of old songs, to which the poem refers, are cries of the Bridegroom seeking and calling out to the bride, as we find in the Song of Songs:

> *Arise, my love, my fair one,*
> *and come away.*
> *O my dove,*
> *in the clefts of the rock,*
> *in the covert of the cliff...*
> *Open to me, my sister, my bride,*
> *my dove, my perfect one;*
> *for my head is wet with dew,*
> *my locks with the drops of the night.*[18]

In this world we live only in imperfect and partial knowledge, obscure and puzzling, and in incomplete and imperfect possession. Contemplation is, as it were, the first–fruits or an earnest given by the Bridegroom: it is a part, not in any way the whole. In that sense man lives in a state of anguish. An anguish that is different from that of existential philosophy; it is the sweet anguish caused by a yearning for God. Instead of being an anguish over the imminence of nothingness, it is a burning desire to possess an All that is felt, and in a certain way, already possessed. But only in a certain way for the time being, which is why the bride still searches and weeps; with the sweet sobbing of lovers, even though, like all weeping, it also involves pain. These themes are best described by poets, like

---

[18]Sg 2: 13–14; 5:2.

the poet author of the Song of Songs. Take, for example, this short poem about the willow, the tree that is said to weep, the weeping willow:

> *Sweet Philomela*
> *is calling her love from the branch*
> *of a green willow at the shady ford.*
> *And the tree feels sorrow*
> *for the bird that cannot find her lover*
> *and that, in her anguish, shouts,*
> *feeling herself burning in sweet flame.*
> *And, from that hour on,*
> *everytime he hears her, the willow also cries.*[19]

That is why contemplative prayer, in this life, not only is compatible with suffering, it in fact demands it in some way. A person who takes Christ seriously has to share in the cross of his Loved One. And that cross will come in all kinds of shapes and sizes. The contemplative man is destined, today more than ever, to feel himself dislodged, out of place, and in the wrong time —vis–à–vis, not only with those outside but also with those within the Church. As

---

[19]In the original:

> *La dulce filomena*
> *llamando está a su amor desde la rama*
> *de verde sauce en el umbroso vado.*
> *Y el árbol siente pena*
> *por el ave que no encuentra a su amado*
> *y que, en su angustia, clama,*
> *sintiendo que se abrasa en dulce llama.*
> *Y, desde aquella hora,*
> *siempre que la oye el sauce, también llora.*

a matter of fact, nobody knows when the world ever thought the contemplative life normal. And we are not referring here to extraordinary mystical phenomena. For a person to suffer rejection all that he need do is take seriously his Christian life so as to act in line with his prayer–life. Or just have real faith, exempt from doubts and anguish: even that will scandalize people. Anyone who dares to adopt an attitude of simple, committed obedience will be accused of practicing outmoded, old–fashioned forms of Christianity. And any priest who is happy in his ministry will probably be regarded with suspicion by other priests who think they have some obligation to feel *anguished* or perhaps *committed*.[20]

No one should be surprised that the contemplative is often regarded as a figure of fun by those around him. Saint Paul said quite clearly that this would happen (2 Tim 3:12). And the bride in the Song seems to be thinking along these lines when, referring to the Bridegroom, she makes this lament:

> *O that you were like a brother to me,*
> *that nursed at my mother's breast!*
> *If I met you outside, I would kiss you,*
> *and none would despise me.*[21]

And yet it is not the jeering that the contemplative finds so painful but, rather, what that jeering implies: it means that he is

---

[20]It would be of interest to explore how this happiness of the contemplative is compatible with how he really does suffer for others. His suffering and concern for the world is at least as great as what *committed* and *anguished* Christians say they feel. One must assume that the suffering the latter experience also comes from true love of God and man, and not from the instability and insecurity of the person's own I. One sometimes gets the impression that underneath this suffering there is nothing but sadness caused, perhaps, by a crisis of faith and generosity.

[21]Sg 8:1.

on his own, that no one wants to love Love. The contemplative feels full solidarity with the rest of men, his brothers, and he loves them more than ever, yet he sees that they are distancing themselves from him. And, although he knows that he has found the right path, he has to watch how others, paying no attention to his cries of warning, take the wrong one that leads them astray, and this causes him an intense suffering that others fail to see, or even suspect. That is why, from time to time, he can even feel sad and tired: he is only human. But he will press ahead, even if it means a big effort, even if he makes slow progress, seeking in all kinds of ways to attain God —like a river which runs its course to the end, until it joins the sea:

> *The sun, already breaking,*
> *with rose colors descends*
> *from the mountain to the slope,*
> *awakening the valley*
> *while I am singing my sorrow.*
>
> *When the chariot of Dawn appears,*
> *the song of the birds,*
> *with a thousand soft trills,*
> *the valley is filling,*
> *while I am singing my sorrow.*[22]

---

[22]In the original:

> *El sol, que ya se asoma,*
> *con rosados colores va bajando*
> *del monte por la loma,*
> *al valle despertando*
> *mientras que yo mi pena voy cantando.*
> *El canto de las aves,*
> *el carro de la Aurora en asomando,*
> *con mil trinos suaves*
> *el valle va llenando,*
> *mientras que yo mi pena voy cantando.*

> *Down the steep slopes*
> *of the mountains, forming torrents,*
> *the river descends*
> *with a soft murmur resounding,*
> *but, finding that no one*
> *answers his song, he sadly takes*
> *a more winding, more tired,*
> *sadder and slower course,*
> *still searching for the sea*
> *while I am singing my sorrow.*[23]

As we have said a number of times, contemplation is only a sort of first–fruits of eternal life. First–fruits bring about joy, because of what they give, but also a kind of pain, because they are only an earnest of something *yet to come*. The contemplative is well aware that he is still on the road. But, given that suffering is the quickest and best road to attain the possession of the Bridegroom, he wants to go out and meet the cross:

---

[23]In the original:

> *Por las altas laderas*
> *de los montes, haciendo torrenteras,*
> *el río va bajando*
> *con un rumor suave resonando;*
> *mas, viendo que a su canto*
> *nadie responde, entristecido tanto,*
> *en curso más sinuoso,*
> *más cansado, más triste y perezoso,*
> *el mar sigue buscando*
> *mientras que yo mi pena voy cantando.*

Awake, O north wind,
and come, O south wind!
Blow upon my garden, let its fragrance be wafted abroad.
Let my beloved come to his garden,
and eat its choicest fruits.[24]

Maybe that wind, by which the soul wants to be shaken, is the wind of suffering. Only then will its fragrance, which is the sweet fragrance of Christ, be able to spread (2 Cor 2:15). The contemplative knows that he needs to link his sacrifice to that of Christ's to make it, too, a *fragrant and sweet–smelling* sacrifice.[25] And he eventually comes to understand what our Lord meant when he said: *Every branch of mine that does bear fruit my Father prunes that it may bear more fruit.*[26]

This passage of the Song can also be taken as meaning that the soul's desire is to feel the gentle breeze of the Spirit, Who is the Wind that breathes wherever He so wishes (Jn 3:8) and Who cannot but bring the sweet fragrance of Christ. A fragrance that is always of the cross, because that is why He came: *For this I have come into the world.*[27]

* * *

---

[24] Sg 4:16.
[25] Eph 5:2.
[26] Jn 15:2.
[27] Jn 18:37.

Contemplative prayer can disappear, which is a further reason why it is compatible with suffering. In this life the Christian condition is always that of a *viator*, a wayfarer. It is true that the mystics speak of certain very elevated states of contemplation, such as spiritual marriage or mystical betrothal; stages when man seems to have some sort of assurance as to the final perseverance of that state. This assurance may be of the same sort as is given by the theological virtue of hope; but here it has been developed to a very high degree. Clearly this is something God can do, because the perfection of love rules out fear of any sort, and therefore the fear of possibly losing that love (1 Jn 4:18). However, particularly if one has not reached those stages, one's assurance can only be fully and absolutely confirmed in Heaven.

The state of contemplative prayer can be lost if the contemplative is unfaithful to the graces received from God. He can regress the whole way, losing all that he has received, or simply go back to less perfect stages of the life of prayer. It is no accident that the bride in the Song compares the Bridegroom to a gazelle or a young stag (Sg 2: 8–9.17) —nervous animals, which are fleet of foot, easily frightened, difficult to see and to hunt, easy to lose sight of, very good at camouflaging themselves, and which come bounding over the hills and leaping upon the mountains of Bether.

> *The voice of my beloved! Behold, he comes,*
> *leaping upon the mountains,*
> *bounding over the hills...*
> *My beloved is like a gazelle, or a young stag...*
> *Turn, my beloved, be like a gazelle,*
> *or a young stag, on the mountains of Bether.*

Contemplative prayer calls for an immediate and generous response on the part of man. He might never hear the voice of the

Bridegroom again, or he might have to wait a long time before he does. This theme is developed in the Song of Songs, where the Bridegroom's call is first heard:

> *Hark! my beloved is knocking,*
> *Open to me, my sister, my love,*
> *my dove, my perfect one...*

But the bride makes excuses and is slow to open:

> *I have put off my garment,*
> *how can I put it on?*
> *I have bathed my feet,*
> *how can I soil them?*

Finally she decides to open to the Bridegroom; but she is too late and He has already gone away:

> *I opened to my beloved,*
> *but my beloved had turned and gone.*
> *I sought him, but found him not;*
> *I called him, but he gave no answer.*
> *The watchmen found me,*
> *as they went about in the city;*
> *they beat me, they wounded me,*
> *they took away my mantle,*
> *those watchmen of the walls.*
> *I adjure you, O daughters of Jerusalem,*
> *if you find my beloved,*
> *that you tell him I am sick with love.*[28]

---

[28]Sg 5: 2–8.

In the life of prayer there is no room for dragging one's feet or putting things off; when God calls man, He expects a generous response. The consequences can be serious. If, having once set out, a person fell back, or, worse still, lost his way, he would be plunged into the deepest sadness. All he would be left with would be the sad memory of a lost paradise and a lost friendship —lost, maybe, forever, like those conch shells, devoid of life, separated from their element for years and years; yet, when one puts them to one's ear, they seem to call up with bitter weeping the memory of the seas and waves that are now lost forever; all that remains is the wind, which somehow evokes, with sad murmurings, times and places that will never return:

> *The sweet breeze, coming down the mountains,*
> *is swaying the poppy fields,*
> *and on reaching the sea, where it bathes,*
> *becomes a murmuring of conch shells*
> *which evokes winds and forgotten waves.*[29]

Our Lord warns us that when we hear the call of divine Love, we must reply immediately: *Be like men who are waiting for their master to come home from the marriage feast, so that they may open to him at once when he comes and knocks. Blessed are those servants whom the master finds awake when he comes; truly, I say*

---

[29]In the original:

> *La suave brisa, desde la montaña,*
> *baja meciendo campos de amapolas,*
> *y llegando hasta el mar, donde se baña,*
> *se convierte en rumor de caracolas*
> *que evocan vientos y olvidadas olas.*

*to you, he will gird himself and have them sit at table, and he
will come and serve them. If he comes in the second watch, or
in the third and finds them so, blessed are those servants.*[30] That
is why our response needs to be rapid: *So that they may open to
him at once when he comes and knocks.* Since the purpose of the
call, the knock, is to give man everything, absolutely everything,
there is no justification for any created thing to get in the way and
keep God waiting. What the part can give, the Whole can bestow
more abundantly. That is why our Lord will not hear of any delay,
any postponement, when it comes to following Him: if one is going
to follow Him once and for all, there is no time for burying one's
father or taking leave of one's family (Lk 9: 59–62). The apparent
exaggeration contained in these divine demands is designed to teach
us something very important: there is no excuse for delay in replying
to God's invitation to follow Him; and still less for saying no to
Him. Besides, our Lord promises happiness to those who respond
generously; twice in the same Gospel passage He describes them as
happy (Lk 12: 37–38). This happiness, promised so emphatically,
depends on man's intimacy with the Lord, an intimacy the Lord
initiates: *Behold I stand at the door and knock; if anyone hears my
voice and opens the door, I will come in to him and eat with him,
and he with me.*[31] Here we can clearly see that reciprocity which will
become friendship, intimacy, love, and relationship between equals:
No longer do I call you servants but friends.[32] In Saint Luke we

---

[30]Lk 12: 36–38.

[31]Rev 3:20. Some modern translations of the Bible tone down the force of this
text by translating it as *and eat together*: thereby losing the sense of intimacy and
reciprocity which comes across in the words *I will eat with him, and he with me.*
Cf. Feuillet, A., *'Jalons pour une meilleure intelligence de l'Apocalypse'*, in *Esprit
et Vie* (1975), p. 216.

[32]Jn 15:15.

find the same, put more strongly, if that were possible: *He will gird himself and have them sit at the table, and he will come and serve them.*

It is not possible to describe the things that are somehow sensed here. Even to attempt to write about them would be sheer temerity. When faced with the intimacy that takes place in contemplation, one must bow before the mystery because words cannot describe what God wants to do with man. Once again we can see clearly that the Christian is someone who has a vocation to happiness; that happiness starts here, because the ineffable world of the supernatural begins for him at baptism. And one must never forget that, as long as one is a wayfarer in this world, this happiness always, necessarily, takes one through the cross.

In this life contemplation will never satiate us. Only in eternal life will it fill man's heart to overflowing. Since, for the time being, contemplation is given as an earnest, *like the fire it never says, Enough.*[33] The contemplative knows that only God can make him happy, even in this life; and he also knows that he never completely possesses Him. The knowledge and love the contemplative attains of Infinitive Goodness, and his awareness that he does not yet fully possess Him, produce in him a mysterious mixture of unspeakable joy and strong yearnings to possess God completely: *I am hard–pressed between the two. My desire is to depart and be with Christ, for that is far better...*[34] These tensions are a feature of contemplative prayer, and, as we have said, they translate into the joy of possessing God and the pain of not possessing Him fully; into desires to consummate one's self–surrender in heaven, and at the same time to continue along the way of the cross: *Yet what I*

---

[33]Prov 30:16.
[34]Phil 1:23.

shall choose I cannot tell, the Apostle confessed.[35] These tensions are contained within a broader one: the feeling of being torn apart and yet at peace; for the contemplative suffers intensely, and, at the same time, he feels and enjoys an interior peace which is the consequence of his abandonment to the divine will. This is the sort of life a contemplative lives. *Abundant* life, as our Lord described it,[36] where man's feelings reach an unbelievable plenitude, where his sensibility (for sorrow and for joy) becomes unimaginably refined, and where man becomes evermore human the more he becomes like God.

---

[35] Phil 1:22.
[36] Jn 10:10.

EPILOGUE

Anyone who tries to talk about prayer, particularly contemplative prayer, runs a rather strange risk: that of discovering when he comes to the end that he has not spoken about prayer at all. At best all that he has done is to talk about things more or less connected with prayer. And yet his effort may still have been worthwhile.

Setting out to talk about God is like setting out to stutter, but if one tries to speak about the sublime things of God, then one is really being daring. Nevertheless, perhaps it will suffice, whether we say much or little about Him. When one talks about God, one always says very little or nothing at all compared with what one ought to have said; and we cannot pretend otherwise.

That is not the only danger, however —the magnitude of the subject as far as God is concerned— there is another hazard, our own deficiency. For, in this area, as nowhere else, a great deal of sincerity and genuineness is called for, and who can claim to know anything about contemplation? Or, what is worse, who can claim that he lives by contemplation? Here again, the sort of interior tearing we spoke about earlier comes into the picture again —very prominently. Contrary to what our Lord said in Saint John's Gospel (Jn 3:11), we speak of what we do not know and bear witness to what we have not seen.

That is true. But man also has a right to live on expectations and nostalgia. What would become of him if it were otherwise? Besides, there will always be someone who can clarify and add. There must be someone who has experienced all this before, and better. And someone who understands it, or can understand it. They will always be those who feel the sweet pain of nostalgia, of the dream of goodness sensed as totality, of truth grasped in clarity, of Love possessed in all its fullness.

Index of Quotations
from the
New Testament

MATTHEW

4: —, **25**

  1, **67**

5: 3, **61**

  4, **72**

  48, **38**

6: 7, **66**

8: 29, **17**

10: 20, **9**, **41**

  38, **61**

11: 27, **92**

13: 19, **35**

  23, **15**, **35**

14: 23, **25**

16: 24, **61**

17: 5, **10**

18: 3, **83**

  4, **83**

25: 6, **27**, **73**

26: 41, 48, **77**

MARK

1: —, **25**

  13, **67**

  35, **25**

4: 20, **35**

6: 31, **29**

8: 34, **61**

  35, **86**

10: 21, **83**

13: 35, **73**

LUKE

4: —, **25**

  1–2, **67**

5: 5, **72**

6: 12, **25**

9: 24, **86**

  59–62, **103**

10: 1, **82**

  4, **83**

  41, **18**

  41–42, **20**

11: 5, **73**

  28, **15**

12: 36–38, **103**

  37–38, **103**

21: 36, **77**

22: 39, **25**

  44, **72**

112

JOHN

1: 4, **86**
  30–31, **82**
3: 8, **11, 34, 99**
  11, **108**
  29, **39, 72**
  34–35, **89**
  35, **89**
4: 10, **38**
  23–24, **40**
  26, **12**
5: 20, **89**
  24, **15**
7: 39, **38**
8: 26, **11**
  43, **18**
  47, **39**
9: 37, **12**
10: 3, **12**
  10, **85, 105**
11: 28, **35**
12: 50, **11**
14: 2, **38**
  6, **38, 84, 86**
  10, **11, 14**
  26, **11, 26**
15: 2, **99**
  5, **39**
  15, **81, 103**
16: 7, **10**

13, **26**
17: 24, **89**
18: 37, **39, 99**

ACTS OF THE APOSTLES

1: 14, **62**
2: 42, **62**
6: 2–4, **18**

ROMANS

4: 18, **73**
6: 4, **62**
8: 5, **55**
  14, **61**
  15–16, **40**
  16, **9**
  26, **9, 39**
  27, **21**

1 CORINTHIANS

2: 10, **21**
  12, **55**
  13, **14**
  14, **41, 55**
  15, **27**

3: 7, **69**
8: 1, **27**
9: 16, **80**
  24, **38**
  26, **38**
12: 3, **39**
  31, **80**
13: —, **80**
  8, **27**
  9–10, **91**
  12, **86**, **92**
  13, **91**
14: —, **80**
  9, **59**
  11, **59**
  18–19, **59**
  19, **80**

2 Corinthians

2: 15, **99**
3: 6, **34**
4: 2, **59**
  11, **62**
6: 10, **72**

Galatians

2: 20, **12**, **35**, **86**
5: 22, **32**, **38**

Ephesians

5: 2, **99**

Philippians

1: 22, **105**
  23, **104**
2: 13, **54**
3: 12–14, **38**
4: 4, **72**

Colossians

1: 24, **62**
3: 4, **86**
  16, **15**

1 Tessalonians

5: 16, **72**
  16–17, **72**

2 Timothy

3: 12, **96**

HEBREWS

1: 1–2, **8**, **10**
5: 7, **72**
10: 5, **87**
11: 1, **91**

JAMES

5: 13, **72**

1 PETER

3: 7, **48**

2 PETER

1: 19–20, **56**
3: 15–16, **56**

1 JOHN

1: 10, **15**
2: 14, **15**
3: 1, **40**
14, **82**, **89**
4: 5, **19**
8, **8**
18, **100**
20, **48**

JUDE

20–21, **40**

REVELATION

1: 15, **12**
2: 23, **21**
26–28, **75**
3: 20, **103**
13: 1–4, **84**
15–17, **84**
22: 16, **75**
18–19, **59**

Contents

PRAYER

Introduction 5

The Bases of Prayer 7

Divine–Human Dialogue and Human Communication 13

Rejection of Prayer and The Crisis of Faith 17

The Practice of Prayer 21

Silence 25

Enemies of Silence: Distractions 31

The Search for Silence: Struggling Against Distractions 33

The Imitation of Christ 37

Mortification and Prayer 43

Meditation and Contemplation Distinguished 51

Prayer and Purification 61

Distractions as an Element of Purification 63

Temptations as an Element of Purification 67

Prayer and The Cross 71

Basic Ideas about Contemplation 77

On The Paths of Contemplation 81

Epilogue 107

www.ingramcontent.com/pod-product-compliance
Lightning Source LLC
Chambersburg PA
CBHW061958090426
42811CB00006B/979